SPANISH DESIGN

AND

ARCHITECTURE

SPANISH DESIGN

AND

ARCHITECTURE

EMMA DENT COAD

RIZZOLI
NEW YORK

Dedicated to the late Charles Dent de Colsa and to
Jaime Fraser-Luckie y Zuleta
without whom this book would never have been attempted

I would like to thank those who helped me in the early stages –
Carlos García-Calvo and Steve Braidwood – and those whose
continued help has made this book possible: José-María Morillo;
Kathy Edmond; Judith Watt; Lucie Young; David Blott; Janet
McNally; Sara Navarro; Alberto Campo Baeza; Deyan Sudjic;
Chris Turner. And special thanks to Juli Capella and Quim Larrea.

First published in the United States of America in 1990 by
RIZZOLI INTERNATIONAL PUBLICATIONS, INC.
300 Park Avenue South, New York, NY 10010

Library of Congress Cataloging-in-Publications Data

Coad, Emma Dent.
    Spanish design and architecture/Emma Dent Coad.
        p.   cm.
    Includes bibliographical references.
    ISBN 0-8478-1173-5
    1. Art, Spanish. 2. Art, Modern–20th century–Spain. I. Title.
N7108.C55 1990
745.4'4946'09048–dc20

Typeset by Litho Link Ltd, Welshpool, Powys, Wales
Printed and bound in Italy

89-28720 CIP

CONTENTS

FOREWORD

Interior from the compact Casa Olerdola, Barcelona, by Jaume Bach and Gabriel Mora, 1981.

In the last decade Spanish design, fashion and architecture have incontestably entered the front rank of the international scene. Supported by a booming domestic economy and the newly liberal climate of the post-Franco era, a distinctive Spanish style has emerged – radical, witty, confident. This book attempts to capture the essence of contemporary Spanish design and architecture but it is always important to see new work in context. Thus, where appropriate, this review begins in the mid-'70s or earlier, but the emphasis in the six main chapters is deliberately placed on the past five years, while the last is a look ahead to 1992. This is the year when the eyes of the world will be turned to Spain for the Olympics, the World Expo, and Madrid's European Cultural Capital celebrations, and the policies and achievements of the Spanish people will be laid out for all to see.

It is impossible to include everyone and everything of importance in a book of finite length. A country of 39 million people which can boast over 300 design shops has more going on than any book could hope to cover. It is also impossible to represent fairly the achievements of all the autonomous regions in their diversity and vigour. I have thus tried to give a selective and balanced view of work across the country, but if the Catalans have achieved more than their fair share of space it is because, like Dali, their excellence at self-publicity has been rewarded.

EMMA DENT COAD

8

INTRODUCTION

'Culture thrives on morality; without, it cannot survive.'

(FRANCISCO FRANCO, 1936)

'The real tragedy for Spain was the death of Mola; there was the real brain, the real leader. Franco came to the top like Pontius Pilate in the Creed. Spain is riddled with clerico-monarchical muck that has floated to the top.'

(ADOLF HITLER, 1937)

Soft construction with Boiled Beans; Premonition of Civil War, *by Salvador Dali, 1936. In his words, 'a vast human body breaking out into monstrous excrescences of arms and legs tearing at one another in a delirium of auto-strangulation', the body being both Spain and Civil War itself. Inspired by the tortured suffering of Goya's war paintings, Dali produced a series on the subject of the looming war. Self-destructiveness, even self-cannibalism, was a frequent theme.*

© DEMART PRO ARTE BV/DACS 1990

The rise of modern Spain from the ashes of the Civil War and the Franco years, has brought the country to the attention of the world. In 15 short years, Spain has passed through a period of economic and political growth that could have taken centuries, and with past restrictions now lifted, its culture has emerged as a virile and potent force comparable to that of many of the Western countries which have been stable for decades.

All credit is due to the Spanish, to their tremendous regional and national pride, their industriousness and eagerness to succeed in the world market. Whatever their politics, the Spanish people have that most elusive characteristic – vision. It is this that has brought about national policies encompassing economic programmes and urban planning schemes to take Spain into the twenty-first century with imaginative and efficient cityscapes that many would not dare to dream of.

The early and middle '80s were years of elation, almost euphoria, among the Spanish themselves, and this was echoed by the foreign media. Many people expected too much too soon: miracles, in this religious country, could still be believed in. But the wheels of democracy are slow. As the years have gone by and some improvements have taken longer than expected, while inevitably mistakes have been made, many Spaniards have become disillusioned. As the country enters the '90s, with the all-important year of 1992 looming, the Spanish people have become altogether more reflective, re-evaluating their objectives and questioning their political leaders. Some Spaniards see the planned events of 1992 – the Barcelona Olympics, the World Expo in Seville, the European Cultural Capital celebrations for Madrid, and the quincentenary festival for Granada – as no more than public-relations exercises, not believing there will be any long-term benefit to the country.

But the countless visitors who will arrive on Spain's doorstep in 1992 will see the whole picture, not just exhibitions, events and festivals. Their Spain will be a heady mixture: the enticing – if polluted – beaches of the Costa del Sol, cool moss-smelling cobbled courtyards, geraniums on windowsills, the exciting designer bars of Madrid and Barcelona, the illiterate goatherd sitting under a tree swigging from a pigskin bottle, Marxist mayors and fusty aristocrats, skinny aloof beauties and Fellini-esque prostitutes. The best and worst of Spain, old and new, will be there for them to explore and fall in love with, and they will carry away an indelible impression of a rich mixture of cultures and lifestyles. Spain, with its many races and languages, invaded dozens of times over thousands of years, has absorbed a wide variety of cultures, all of which have helped to form its own spirit, hard to define but very much in evidence today.

SPAIN'S ARTISTIC HERITAGE

Spanish civilization began in the Stone Age, and the country not only has countless fine buildings and artefacts, but has also produced a disproportionate number of the most famous painters in the world and has inspired generations of artists from abroad to create their best work. In Roman times Mérida was the centre of the country: called 'the second Rome', it produced art objects many of which equalled or surpassed those of Rome itself. Under the Visigoths, in the sixth century, Spain emerged as an independent kingdom, with Toledo as its capital, rivalling Italy in civilization, law and the sciences as well as in architecture, decoration and metalwork. Half a century after the Muslim conquest in 711 Córdoba, the glittering new capital, had a million inhabitants, and was grander than Baghdad or Byzantium. Muslim art and architecture reached their peak in the tenth and eleventh centuries, and when Seville became the capital under the Almohades, the beautiful and emblematic tower, La Giralda, now incorporated into the cathedral, was built. The Alhambra at Granada is the only secular complex to survive from the Muslim Middle Ages.

Some medieval Mozarabic art (so called from the name given to Spaniards who kept to their Christian religion and traditions under Muslim rule) is probably the closest there is to a vernacular style of the time. When Alfonso VI captured Toledo in 1085, he brought with him

Set on a hill with precipitous slopes, the buildings which make up the Alhambra in Granada dominate the town. Begun in the eleventh century, very little of the original structures exist apart from walls restored in the sixteenth century; however, as the seat of the Sultanate for five hundred years, it contains some of the finest examples of Moorish art in the world.

11

INTRODUCTION

Las Meninas *by Diego Velázquez,*
1656. The Infanta Margarita is
prepared by her ladies-in-waiting to
be painted by the artist in his studio in
the palace, watched from behind the
viewer by his patron, Philip IV, who is
reflected in a mirror. Elements of
luxury, formality and the grotesque
are at work in this interior – some say
the best in the world – painted at a
time when Spain was losing both
territory and power.

French artists and sculptors, and the French monastic orders who followed him also brought their own architects and craftsmen. This was the beginning of a long period during which there was no opportunity for any indigenous Spanish style to emerge.

The fourteenth and fifteenth centuries saw the building of many glorious Franco-Spanish cathedrals. Queen Isabella, at the end of the fifteenth century, collected Flemish art, importing work by Gérard David, and German and Flemish architects were also invited to Spain to work on churches and cathedrals, including Seville Cathedral. An 'Isabellan' style evolved, which was a peculiar combination of Germanic and Muslim influences.

In the sixteenth century, Italy began to dominate Spanish art, architecture and design, with the Venetian influence particularly strong. This Renaissance period was a prolific one in architecture. The royal architects Juan Bautista de Toledo and Juan de Herrera both visited Michelangelo's Rome, bringing back a new austere style which they applied to such buildings as the Escorial, the palace built for Philip II in Madrid. Painters of the time, like Luís de Vargas, worked in a cold Mannerist style, exemplified by *La Gamba* in Seville Cathedral, but polychromed wood, disdained in Italy, once again became popular in Spain.

Philip II, with his fantastic wealth pouring in from the Americas, was a connoisseur and collector of paintings, the patron of some of Spain's greatest artists, as well as of Titian, Tintoretto and Veronese. He looked less favourably on the visionary style of the extraordinary El Greco ('The Greek'), Domenikos Theotokopolous, who adopted Spain as his country, but whose one commission from the king was rejected. Realism gradually took over from Mannerism, with its chief exponent José de Ribera influenced by Francisco Zurbarán, whose marvellous, austere paintings of monks and ascetics were executed mainly for the religious orders. Diego Velázquez and Bartolomé Esteban Murillo, both from Seville, moved to Madrid to be near Philip's new capital, bringing with them the softened mellow sunlit tones of Seville.

In the seventeenth century, as ever, the Spanish craftsman's empathy with wood made itself felt again. Realistic polychromed wooden sculpture became increasingly popular, at the expense of Italian marbles and the heroic figures influenced by Michelangelo. Painted-wood statues of saints were paraded on feast days on *pasos* (floats), dressed in rich costumes and decked in jewellery donated by the faithful.

In the eighteenth century the Bourbon dynasty brought in yet more foreign artists, this time the French, and the Neoclassical style began to appear in Spain. In the fine arts, the dominant figure towards the end of the century was Francisco de Goya, whose work was often critical and ironic, and whose soul-searching portraits are among the finest and most penetrating ever produced. Sensitive and highly imaginative, Goya was deeply stirred by the scenes of war and bloodshed he had witnessed, and in his later years painted a nightmarish series of pictures on the walls of his house near Madrid.

BELOW Verres, Journal et
Bouteille de Vin, *by Juan Gris.*
With Georges Braque and Picasso,
Gris was one of the first Cubists, living
near Picasso in Montmartre, Paris.
This early collage is typical of his style
and soft colouring which were so
unlike that of the others. His death at
the age of 40 robbed the world of a
great master.
© DACS 1990

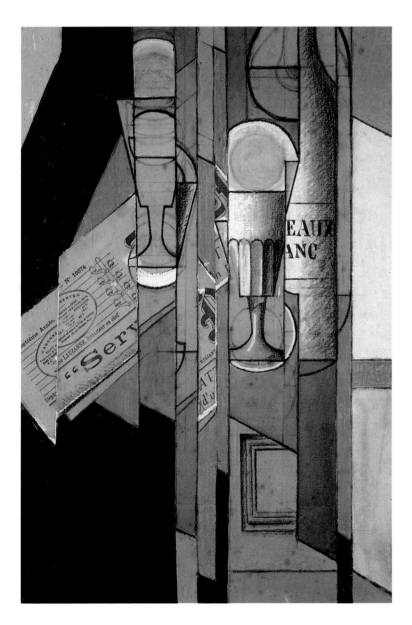

ABOVE Jacqueline in a Mantilla
on a Red Background, *by Pablo*
Picasso. Picasso married the model
Jacqueline Roque in 1958, when he
was well into his seventies and living
comfortably in the South of France.
With the troubled days of Guernica
and the more aggressive side of
Cubism behind him, he has painted a
relaxed domestic portrait.
© DACS 1990

13

INTRODUCTION

Aidez l'Espagne *by Joan Miró*
1937. Poster calling for help from the
French for Republican Spain. The
inscription says: 'In the current
struggle, I see on the fascist side
outdated troops, and on the other side
the people, whose great creative
resources will give Spain an impetus
which will astonish the world.' Photo
Lauros-Giraudon-Bridgeman.

14

Art in nineteenth-century Spain echoed that of the rest of Europe. Churches were built in the neo-Gothic style and official buildings in the Romanesque or Classical idiom. Much of the painting was in the easily accessible narrative manner popular in Victorian England, with the Pre-Raphaelite and Art Nouveau reactions to this making an impact in their turn.

In the early twentieth century an eccentric and unique movement began to gain pace in Catalonia, fired by Cubism, Futurism and Dadaism. The so-called Generation of '29, the Surrealist movement encompassing writers, artists, photographers and sculptors, was moulded in the discussions held in the cafés of Barcelona. The artists Pablo Picasso, Juan Gris, Joan Miró and Salvador Dali, the film-maker Luís Buñuel and the poet and musician Federico García Lorca all began to find their voices, sometimes collaborating in bizarre performances or exhibitions. Dali's work with Buñuel produced a series of brief films, the best known of which, *Un Chien Andalou*, contains allusions and allegories so subtle as to be barely perceptible. Always the most controversial figure in the movement, the wilfully anarchic Dali antagonized his contemporaries by staying in Spain after Franco's victory when most of the others had fled to Paris. He also either disgusted the art world or won its fervent admiration by publicizing both his work and his lifestyle, much as Andy Warhol did in the '60s and '70s. The death of this extraordinary figure in Barcelona in 1988 was felt almost as keenly as that of Antoni Gaudí over 50 years before.

ABOVE AND BELOW *Two scenes from the Surrealist film* Un Chien Andalou *by Luís Buñuel and Salvador Dali, filmed in the inspiring and freer atmosphere of France. This was one of a series of allegorical films by this partnership, echoing the repression of the time and warning of the impending civil war.*

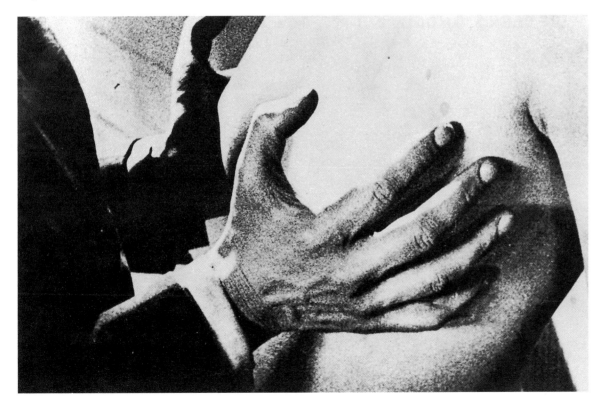

INTRODUCTION

LA MOVIDA

As late as 1975, Spain was a repressed country where the bikini was still banned, but within five years it had thrown itself into an orgy of hedonism reminiscent of high-spirited teenagers with their first cars and front-door keys. Night clubs, bars, sex shows and general promiscuity flourished unashamedly for the first time, and the new atmosphere of openness and experimentation gave a powerful impetus to the arts in particular. These were the years of La Movida – a slang expression for what is current, 'where it's at' or, literally, 'the movement' – begun by a collection of avant-garde writers, painters, rock musicians, philosophers, fashion designers, photographers, indeed anyone involved in the arts or interested in their progress.

The group Alaska y Dinarama produced punk rock music which made them as popular as the Beatles had been in the '60s, while Agatha Ruíz de la Prada designed extraordinary experimental clothes, many of them unwearable. Ouka Lele began her career of taking strange, other-worldly staged photographs; Pedro Almodóvar made films which reflected the crazy pace of living at the time, choosing as his actors the beautiful or bizarre 'stars' of the movement. In 1985 he expressed the spirit of La Movida: 'The people born in the late '50s and early '60s don't think about the past . . . We are free, we are alive, we don't know where we're going but we're full of excitement.' His film of the same year, *What have I done to deserve this?*, a black comedy of Madrid working-class life, made an impact in Spain and the rest of Europe, but most particularly in New York, while his 1989 film, *Women on the verge of a nervous breakdown*, was similarly acclaimed and received nominations for an Oscar.

16

TOP LEFT *De Negro (on black) by Alfonso Fraile, 1986. One of a series of rather brutal portraits by this Sevillian painter. The lack of background or anything which gives perspective forces concentration on the face.*

CENTRE *Summer 1987 outfit by Agatha Ruíz de la Prada, very much a prime mover in La Movida, and still producing clothing to shock and challenge.*
ABOVE *Extraordinary wired dress by Madrileño Manuel Piña. This dress, designed at the height of La Movida in 1983, shows Piña's sense of theatre.*

Cover and inside page of Borja Casani's Sur Exprés *magazine. Each issue is on a theme, this one being the quote, 'In the kingdom of the blind'*

(the one-eyed man is king). Extensive use of colour illustration is a feature of Emilio Gil's design for the magazine.

La Movida was far from being exclusive to the inner-city intellectual élite; it quickly spread throughout Spanish society, capturing the imaginations of young people in working-class suburbs, who adapted the styles to suit their tastes. The mouthpieces of the movement were magazines like *La Luna de Madrid*, *Madrid Me Mata* and Barcelona's *Primera Linea*, focusing on the work and lifestyles of Spain's creative leaders. A television programme, *La Edad de Oro*, showed artists' work and discussed their private lives with unprecedented frankness. Proof that ordinary Spanish people are just as interested in their environment as designers themselves was provided by the great success of the magazine *El Croquis*, a glossy architectural quarterly. Of these magazines, Borja Casani's *La Luna* has now become the less manic but still avant-garde *Sur Exprés*, while *El Croquis* gave birth first to *De Diseño*, then to *ARDI* magazine, both edited by Juli Capella and Quim Larrea.

The movement's painters have also seen much success. These New Expressionists, or New Figurationists, among them Guillermo Perez Villalta, Sigfrido Martin Begué, José María Sicilia and Luís Gordillo, express the vibrancy of their time, taking elements of comic-strip humour or satire of the Spanish old masters as their starting points. Many, like Almodóvar, deal in Spain's favourite currency of irony, catching up on the social comment and criticism forbidden for so many years. A considerable spur for these painters has been the Spaniards' genuine enthusiasm for art collecting: they could actually sell their work. More recently, US art lovers have also begun to invest in modern Spanish painting and sculpture.

DESIGN IN THE NEW SPAIN

1984 was a peak year for Spain. More tourists than ever before flocked to the country, rivalling the indigenous population in numbers, and at the same time exports grew by an astonishing 30 per cent. This influx of money funded a huge programme of modernization for the national transport network. A second Arab invasion began when King Fahd of Saudi Arabia built himself a summer residence – a replica of the White House – in the environs of Marbella. A programme for the modernization of traditional industries such as steel, shipbuilding and textiles was virtually completed, and a long-term scheme was set up to encourage high-tech industries around Madrid. The economy was improving steadily: industrial production in Barcelona had doubled since 1970, and Gross National Product per capita doubled between 1980 and 1986. But increased mechanization took its toll, and unemployment was still high at 21 per cent, with nearly half of the mainly Andalucian workforce, one and a half million of whom had migrated to Catalonia during the '60s boom, losing their jobs. Further schemes to update other areas of industry and reduce unemployment are paramount in the government's plans.

The vertiginous pace of growth slowed down in early 1988, rather to the relief of some manufacturers, who were beginning to doubt their ability to meet increasing foreign orders without major investment programmes which they might not yet be ready for. The economy has slowly begun to improve again since then, and the festivities planned for 1992 present bright prospects for tourism as well as for industry, transport, banking and business in general.

However, the Single European Market, which will become operational the same year, will be the start of the open season, with international companies operating on the same footing as Spanish ones. Seat, a major earner in Spain's national car industry – the fourth largest in Europe – split from its parent company Fiat in the early '80s, and has already been sold to VW/Audi after using Italian designers for some years. Foreign design consultancies with impressive experience in design, research and marketing have opened offices in Spain and won major contracts in competition with Spanish designers, while British and American companies have been especially quick in seeing the potential of the Spanish market for their kind of expertise. Specialist back-up companies such as photo-composition and photography laboratories, printers and sign-makers, model-makers and typesetters, especially those needing major investment in high-tech equipment, are also setting up in Spain, bringing in their own employees. The credits list of Expo '92 will be as telling as the exhibits in the international pavilions.

Industrial design, the lifeblood of a healthy economy, is at present the weakest link in the chain. During the 40 years of Franco's rule, manufacturers were encouraged to make cheap copies of goods from abroad, and since imports were severely restricted, they had a virtual monopoly. Design research and development were in some areas actually

17

INTRODUCTION

prohibited by law, leading to an over-protected and retrogressive industrial base. Today many large manufacturers are still extremely staid, reluctant to take risks or do anything involving heavy investment. This situation is alleviated to some extent by the government's expansion programmes (including interest-free loans for purchase of capital equipment) and the encouragement of BCD (Barcelona Centro de Diseño). Various schemes have been set up to subsidize a certain amount of design consultancy time, and courses arranged for those within industry to find out how to improve competitiveness and quality, the latter being the main objective for Spanish manufacturers.

The tidal wave of media attention given to the fashion designers of La Movida has now been transferred to the more serious and established designers. The Spanish strengths in tailoring, colour and the production of high-quality, interesting and wearable clothes have been encouraged by the government, and fashion clothing has become a flourishing and virile industry. The rather sleazy and 'artistically worthy' basements and warehouses where the moving spirits of La Movida met are now chic venues epitomizing the stylish new face of Spain, places where the well-dressed proudly bearing 'Made in Spain' labels meet in designed interiors surrounded by the furniture of the country's top designers.

There are those who believe that this commercialism is the beginning of the end, a first step to the internationalization of design which could result in a characterless 'Euro-design' style. As Juli Capella says, 'Architects, designers and artists in Spain are as yet uncontaminated by the crushing homogeneity which exists elsewhere and which makes the shop windows, bars, furniture, paintings and products of London at times barely distinguishable from those of New York, Paris, Tokyo and the rest of consumer society.' The 'as yet' is the point of contention. Industrial designer Josep Lluscà does not believe it will ever happen, as Spain has its own contribution to make. 'We do not need a big false story like Memphis in Italy to stir up the pot. We do have something new and

RIGHT *The face of new Spain dressed by one of the country's best loved designers, Pedro del Hierro, who is barely known outside Spain. This is his autumn 1989 look for men. Photo by Miguel Oriola.*

CENTRE *Bon Drap is one of Spain's top upholstery fabric manufacturers, who commissions fashion designers to produce designs for them. The one in this elegantly styled photograph is by Vicente Mateu. Photo by Zaibi.*

18

The delicate hues obtainable in silk have inspired Madrid designer Jesús del Pozo in his spring/summer 1989 collection. Natural shoulder lines and a long slim waist with billowing skirts are classic Spanish shapes. Seville orange and this pale apricot colour occur frequently. Photo by Paco Rubio.

important to say.'

Others see this very contemporaneity as a threat to their personal vision of Spain, as though the country were a comforting, lace-making grandmother dressed in widow's black who suddenly inherits a fortune and takes up the habits thought of as the unique preserve of youth. Such people want the world to see the 'real' Barcelona, with its prostitutes, begging drug addicts and backstreet bars where knife-fights are an everyday event, before it is 'ruined' by being cleaned up. Yet others see the changes being made as a natural sign of progress of a country in metamorphosis. Norberto Chaves says that 'The sudden stardom of design is not, as many believe and others would wish, a "fashion", but rather a symptom of a process of change in the consumer society.' (*Art Book II*, Pigmalion, 1985.)

TRADITION AND THE SPANISH OUTLOOK

Spain has a tradition of the coexistence of past and present. The idea of tradition fighting modernity, as if one were preferable to the other, prevalent among American and British architects, designers and critics, seldom arises. Perhaps this is an Anglo-Saxon trait: in France and Italy there is and always has been a proper appreciation of tradition. As Francis Ambrière asks, 'Does not a sincere respect for tradition consist of knowing how to adapt to an ever-changing world while remaining faithful to the principles that went to make up the true values of our labours?' (Introduction to *Spain*, Hachette World Guides series, Librairie Hachette, 1961.)

The insistence on keeping up traditions can be hard for the more developed Western countries to accept, particularly when applied to cultural rather than artistic activities. Antoñete, Madrid's most famous bullfighter, returned to the ring in 1986 after retirement because he saw a renewed interest. 'I've been very surprised by the recognition from the young, which undoubtedly signifies a revitalization of the fiesta. This is specially significant after a long epoch, after the return of the democracy, when it was widely believed that the world of bullfighting was a reactionary one.' Antoñete's justification of the *corrida* springs from the Spanish belief in the worthiness of a glorious death, the freedom to die honourably rather than live in drudgery. 'The *toro bravo* has a strong, agile, athletic constitution, with a type of muscle structure corresponding to his nature. This unique race reaches its complete realization in the culminating moment of the fiesta, at the moment of truth, the moment of death. In the old days, they were all tame, when there were so many ox-carts. This is the real cruelty, to be tied, dragging a cart full of stones.'

There are many other Spanish customs which will never die, for instance that of meeting friends just to discuss or argue, known as *la tertulia*. The Spanish are a highly critical race, a fact which may surprise some people who have experienced another Spanish trait, that of flattery. *La tertulia* is a gathering of friends, very often a regular weekly or monthly

INTRODUCTION

event, and nowadays politics is often on the agenda. But as Luís Carandell, writer and specialist in Spanish customs, says: 'Logical reasoning and conventional analysis are taboo. What really count are wit and a flair for the outlandish ... The philosophy of the *tertulia* is usually heretical ... It is customary to speak badly of the absent, and gossip is the main reason for attending.' Thought to have had its origins in Madrid, this kind of argument as an intellectual exercise is common around the country, a healthy habit throughout all strata of Spanish society. It is not purely the province of writers and intellectuals, architects and designers, but the constant self-questioning of the intelligentsia certainly contributes to the depth, vitality, expressiveness and lack of complacency in the work produced.

The strongest tradition of all, of course, is religion, and there is a constant tension between the forces of modern life and the Spanish people's deeply ingrained Catholicism. Among artists and designers there are several recluses, ascetics and celibates, and their forebear Antoni Gaudí was all of these things. The manner of Franco's death can be seen as a symbol of the way Spain has been wrenched into the twentieth century. Lying in the most modern clinic surrounded by Spain's best doctors, he was wired up to every conceivable medical device, coaxing his failing body to last a little longer. But just in case a miracle could be achieved, his body was covered by the mantle of the Virgin of Pilar, and he held the mummified arm of St Teresa of Avila. Another example is provided by a penitent who was explaining the customs of Holy Week before Easter, and the kind of repentance many Catholics indulge in. This can include walking through the streets – sometimes on their knees – carrying on their shoulders heavy *pasos* (floats) covered in candles, flowers and statues of saints. 'If I do that at Easter,' the penitent explained, 'I can sin for the rest of the year.' Although church-going has declined in Spain, the Catholic guilt system is alive and well.

The irony of the penitent's comment was, of course, deliberate. Irony is Spain's favourite type of humour, a playful but serious comment on their life and work which the Spanish are the first to criticize. A word which frequently comes up in conversation or writing about design is *ludico* (playful), and it is that subtly measured element of jokiness or absurdity integrated into serious design which gives it its special character. Metaphor and allegory are also present at times, but never prevent work being understood on its basic level as well. For example, many furniture designers name their work after past masters who may have inspired them, and a piece may make allusions to this without resorting to pastiche. But it can also stand on its own without any explanation. Seeing things at two levels is another characteristic of the Spanish mentality. Since Franco's days, when his version of morality was imposed even if it meant the destruction of works of art, when political or social comment was frowned upon if not actually banned, the use of allegory has assumed extra importance. In a land where the Marx Brothers' films were forbidden and the word 'thigh' was struck from a theatre script by the censors for being too suggestive, authors,

playwrights and film-makers had to tread warily.

Other words which come up frequently when Spaniards discuss design and architecture are *lirico* and *poetico*. The passionate and romantic Latin temperament is evident in their work, and so is the fact that designers, like all Spaniards, have a thirst for learning and culture. Many designers studied fine art, philosophy or architecture before discovering their true interests and talents.

Spain is a country composed of many separate and different regions, and regional distinctions are perceptible in design as they are in character. The Madrileños tend to be slightly tight-lipped and formal, the Catalans hedonistic and resolutely anarchic, the Basques determined and business-like, the Galicians cool and introspective, and the Andalucians sensual and leisurely. While they are all Spanish, they are first and foremost loyal to their regions, and this obviously influences everything they do.

For an outsider, it can be difficult to understand the industrial make-up of the country, but the amount each autonomous region contributes to the Gross National Product is revealing. The figures are Catalonia 20 per cent; Madrid region 14.8 per cent; Andalucía 13.2 per cent; Valencia region 10 per cent; Basque Country 6.9 per cent; and Galicia 6 per cent. In terms of area and population, the Basques, whose strange language is of unknown origin, contribute more per square mile than any other. The historic rivalry between Madrid and Barcelona can be more readily grasped when you realize that, although Madrid is the capital city, Catalonia has half as many again of both inhabitants and industrial production as Madrid region.

SPONSORSHIP AND THE ARTS

Today art and design, like many cultural activities in Spain, are highly politicized. Politicians like to be associated with prestigious cultural events, either by initiating them, ensuring funds are made available for them, or by making public appearances at them. Sponsorship of the arts by private companies is also extremely healthy. In many countries established and respectable organizations prefer to sponsor classical art, ballet or theatre, but in Spain they are happy to be seen supporting avant-garde exhibitions or events. Reliance on the stability of old-established art forms does not figure highly.

Indeed some people are afraid that institutions are giving their support to virtually any art movement with little regard for intrinsic qualities. The arts magazine *Arena* commented as follows on the plans for new arts centres in Andalucía: 'It is quite clear that the main preoccupation is to leave a political mark on the building. No thought is given as to how to create in Seville or Granada an intelligent space where artistic events may flourish. What matters is to appear intelligent by creating a centre which indicates in a monumental way the flourishing of political developments.' There seems to be a danger that art is being created specifically for

Annunciation *by Domenikos Theotokopolous, known as El Greco (the Greek). The painter left his native Crete for Spain and lived in Toledo until his death in 1614. Perhaps the most inspirational religious painter, El Greco produced strange, angular and elongated forms which perfectly express the intensity of Spanish Catholicism.*

Oscar Tusquets' Gaulino chair, designed as a tribute to Antoni Gaudí and to Italian designer Carlo Mollino, using elements from the work of both. The chairs are produced entirely by hand using traditional craft techniques, giving credibility to this striking hybrid. Photo by Ferran Freixa.

museums, purposely to attract sponsorship. As *Arena* sees it, 'The low cultural level, the most wretched of Franco's legacies, cannot be corrected by sheer bombardment of artistic and intellectual fashions. The young are being exploited to represent the energy the political system wishes to associate itself with.'

Not everybody shares this view and in art, as in design, Spain has many admirers. In terms of trade, West Germany, France (where most of Spain's tourists originate), the USA, the UK, Italy and Japan in that order are putting their money where their admiration lies. Cultural-exchange exhibitions of all kinds are also becoming more popular, and will be even easier logistically after the Single European Market in 1992. Links between art and design colleges are being forged, with student placements becoming a regular feature. Student competitions between European colleges are also becoming more common, with the Spanish willingness to learn French or Italian being a major advantage.

Progress always has its casualties, and one possible result of the new, more structured and technically based design courses could be an end to the interdisciplinary nature of design that has characterized Spain for so long. New technology may enable progress to be made in specialist fields, but it could also exclude those who might previously have been able to add their own idiosyncracies to a design discipline: that most prolific designer, Javier Mariscal, trained in graphic design, and when designing furniture borrows the expertise of industrial designer Pepe Cortés for the technical aspects. It would be tragic if the valuable input of artist/ designers was lost in the rush to become commercial. Fortunately, the numbers of collaborations between complementary talents in different fields – perhaps a result of the continuing habit of *tertulias* – show no sign yet of dwindling. Even at an official level, art and design are brought together. Joan Miró designed the symbol for the Spanish Tourist Office, the sculptor Eduardo Chillido the logo for the Centro de Arte Reina Sofía, while Mariscal as a cartoonist was chosen to produce an Olympic mascot. Fashion designers and carpet manufacturers alike ask painters to produce designs, while many designers and architects devote part of their time to serious painting. For what such practices contribute to the richness and vitality of Spanish design and architecture, long may they last.

Brochure cover for the Centro de Arte Reina Sofía with logo by the sculptor Eduardo Chillido. Madrid's major arts centre was undergoing major alterations only eighteen months after it opened.

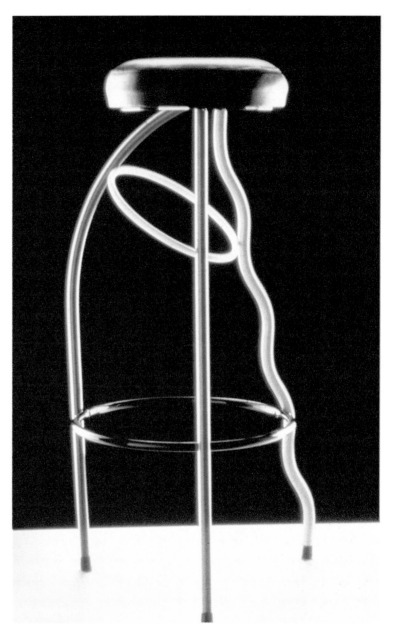

The very graphic lines of Pepe Cortes and Javier Mariscal's Duplex bar stool, for furniture manufacturer Akaba, include an unexpected twist.

23

INTRODUCTION

24

ARCHITECTURE

'They know, without speaking of pertinence, how to produce an architecture that is rooted in its own culture, and how, without speaking of regionalism, to firmly plant an architecture in its own surroundings, how to convey what is current without plagiarizing.'

(ALBERTO CAMPO BAEZA, *YOUNG SPANISH ARCHITECTURE*, ARK ARCHITECTURAL PUBLICATIONS, 1985)

TOP *Façade of Antoni Gaudí's unfinished church of La Sagrada Familia. Gaudí's fascination for Gothic architecture, of which there is an abundance in Barcelona, can be seen in the towering pinnacles, proportions, and in the profusion of carved stonework.*

OPPOSITE, BELOW *Gaudí's bridge, made of rough-hewn stones put together without mortar.*

One of the signs of a developed civilization is the state of its architecture. As a legacy of centuries of invasion, Spain has a tremendous wealth of ancient buildings of contrasting character – Primitive Christian, Roman, Visigothic, Moorish, Mudejar – followed by five centuries of buildings with their roots in the strong artistic alliances with France and Italy. Spain seems to have charged the ancient architects with a vitality unknown in their native countries. Some of the best examples of Roman and of Moorish architecture were conceived in Spain, and much of the material evidence is still standing today. The country is a living museum of architecture, and this has deeply influenced modern practitioners, who have a wide and impressive vocabulary at their disposal as well as an innate feeling about the complementary coexistence of buildings of different periods. These architects, with the active encouragement of their clients, have the opportunity to use this knowledge adventurously, producing expressive architecture which works at many different levels.

Over the centuries there have been many threats to the establishment of a Spanish vernacular style. For example, when the wealthy Austrian Bourbon dynasty acceded to the throne in 1700 Philip V drafted in French craftsmen to build his palace, while his successor called upon Venetians to decorate it. The Venetian Neoclassical style was directly opposed to the movement towards realism popular at the time with Spanish artists and craftsmen, but the Venetians overwhelmed them. Even that most Spanish of sports, bullfighting, which is (to foreigners) synonymous with Spain, was originally a Phoenician import, and bullrings were and still are built with Moorish influence. Does this make them more or less Spanish? There is constant debate about whether this factor depletes or enriches Spanish artistic culture, but there can be no definitive answer to such questions.

25

THE BACKGROUND

From the beginning of the nineteenth century, Spain was building in a grand but unadventurous Gothic and Romanesque revival style, as elsewhere in Europe. But a Catalan cultural revival, originally sparked off by a group of poets in the 1820s, was to change all this. It fired the imagination of the best known of Spanish architects, Antoni Gaudí, who dramatically altered both the face and the image of Barcelona, and eventually became the figurehead of the movement. Gaudí's well-known and well-loved buildings, furniture and wrought-iron work were touched with the romanticism of the Art Nouveau movement which was sweeping Europe towards the end of the century, but had none of its

domesticity. He was passionately religious to the point of asceticism. In his daily life he was being both celibate and reclusive, a not uncommon combination among highly creative Spanish men, even today.

There is a complex philosophical rationale behind Gaudí's work which, perhaps like that of William Morris, was more important though less enduring than the decorative style he is remembered for. His famous Güell Park was a small part of an ambitious plan to build a whole village for working-class families, a utopian dream which obsessed him totally as the years went by, at the expense of his other work. Unlike Morris' naive rural style, however, Gaudí's work is dangerous, impossible, defiant. It is fired by the destructive self-abnegation of Catholicism at its worst and by the Catalan ferocity for life. The people of Barcelona worshipped him for

it. This Catalan spirit, which was later to be seen in the work of the artists Joan Miró, Juan Gris and Salvador Dali, is very much alive today, and is one of the factors in the transformation of Barcelona into a city able to offer visitors to the 1992 Olympic Games a wealth of cultural as well as functional amenities.

The Franco years, especially the early more repressive period, produced very conservative architecture, and the freedom of the former eclecticism all but disappeared. Though certain elements of this were kept, faith in the International Style of Mies van der Rohe and Walter Gropius was all but lost, and the decorative qualities of Art Deco were seen as inappropriate and frivolous. What little building was undertaken took its cue from Italian and German Fascist architecture. A period of heroic or epic architecture followed, perhaps partly inspired by Franco's fascination with Hollywood films.

In the late '60s and early '70s, Franco encouraged a tourist boom, and allowed unrestricted development along sections of the Mediterranean coast, especially the Costa del Sol. Hastily thrown up hotels and apartment blocks, many now in sad disrepair, are his legacy there, but fortunately the '60s building boom was more or less restricted to this area. Spain never suffered the same scale of development across the country as did some other European countries, where decaying tower blocks and city centres are now being demolished. With some notable exceptions, this period of stagnation lasted until the early '70s, when architects around the world became obsessed with a style inspired by

The Miró Centre of Contemporary Art, architect José-Luís Sert, 1972/75. The elegant Miró Foundation building, which houses the Joan Miró collection, watches over Barcelona from its terraced perch in the hills of Montjuïc Park, near the Olympic stadium. Its timelessness, calm spacious interiors and white exterior recall the work of Mies van der Rohe, whose 1929 pavilion has been rebuilt nearby (see LEFT and page 46).

27

ARCHITECTURE

technology. This became the new international language. In Spain it coincided with a loosening of government restrictions on trade, which brought some money into the country.

To some extent architectural culture in Spain runs parallel to that of Italy and close to that of the United States, but the years of imposed isolation have given it a different and more introspective character. The Spanish, while watching the progress of great architects from other countries, have chosen a divergent path. Elsewhere, the battle between the forces of innovation and the forces of convention is a constant one, but the Spanish character is able to tolerate their co-existence, and this is especially evident in the sympathetic restoration, conversion or extension of ancient buildings.

Paradoxically, Spain has benefited from a long period when architectural projects – especially those offering any degree of creative freedom – were scarce. Many architects encountered such economic difficulties during the Franco years that they were forced to stop practising, becoming instead theorists and teachers. Now that the opportunities to build are many and varied, they and their students have turned this period of retrenchment to advantage, and their work is more thoughtful and expressive as a result. Architectural commentators are hypercritical and highly sceptical, and debate, between peers or in the architectural reviews – *Arquitectura*, *El Croquis* and *Quaderns* – can be serious and even fierce. This level of criticism has bred quality, and in the '80s the eyes of the architectural world turned to Spain more and more often. Spanish issues of major international architectural magazines and exhibitions on the subject are common, and Spanish practitioners are invited to lecture at top architectural schools.

What has made this generation so special? As Kenneth Frampton explains in his introduction to *Young Spanish Architecture* (Ark Monograph, 1985), the current generation have inherited the 'delicacy, lucidity and elegance of Oiza's Banco de Bilbao' and the 'cultivated vibrance of Moneo's Bankinter'. These two seminal works of the early '70s were produced from the same stable, that of Francisco Javier Saenz de Oiza and his pupil Rafael Moneo respectively, and owed much to rationalism. The organic or eclectic rationalism of the '80s, especially of the Madrid architects, produces monumental work that is softer and more human than the original rationalists' work. For this generation, says Frampton, 'building remains an act of consummate poetic power'. Building in the large rather than in the small scale, these architects create buildings that are mysterious, beautiful and authoritative, appealing to the cultural nature of a race which does not like to be underestimated. They build for permanence, rejecting nostalgia, folkloric solutions or narrative themes which could soon become outdated. The architectural homogeneity and instant gratification of mass consumerist society has not yet taken over. The pessimists say that eventually it will; others believe that Spanish architects may continue to combine technical high quality and permanence, in buildings which are uncompromisingly modern but never faddish.

28

Producing a critical survey of contemporary Spanish architecture creates many problems, one of which is that there is simply so much of it. And a large proportion of it is worthy of analysis. Spain has ten schools of architecture in six of the autonomous regions around the country, which produce an impressive 1000 graduates a year in a population of 39 million. This compares with just 800 in the United Kingdom's population of 55 million. Since the early '80s, there has been a tremendous amount of building, rebuilding and restoration work going on in Spain. Some is commercial or private work arising from the new prosperity of the country, some is concerned with long-overdue social and educational projects sponsored by the government, and some is connected with preparations for 1992, when three events, the Barcelona Olympics, the World Expo in Seville and the Madrid European Cultural Capital of the Year celebrations will bring visitors flooding into the country.

THE 1970s

The early years of the decade produced some great works which, while they may not accord with current aesthetic taste, are still admired for their technical brilliance. Franco's reign encouraged the power and wealth of banking institutions, which have almost everywhere been traditionally linked to patronage of the best architects. The mighty Bankinter on the Paseo de la Castellana in Madrid, by Rafael Moneo and Ramòn Bescos (1973, completed 1976), combined age-old necessities with the latest technology. It was conceived from the inside out, taking the people, their business and their objects as the starting point. Every fourth floor is a pillarless open space; the four floors above are supported by girders branching out from a central structure. The style is monumental, with allusions to Alvar Aalto, but it is more organic and represents a real departure from the more formally stark International Style corporate buildings along most of the Paseo de la Castellana, of which there are many. Moneo's apprenticeship with Saenz de Oiza, architect of the much admired Banco de Bilbao, famous landmark of Madrid, is evident in his design of the Bankinter. Another architectural landmark of the '70s is Javier Carvajal's Banco Adriatico, built in the same area of Madrid as the Banco de Bilbao.

Moneo's Ayuntamiento de Logrono (1973, completed 1981) combines urban imperatives with modern architectural features, and is more contextual than his earlier work. An architectural signpost of its period is the Colegio de Arquitectos de Sevilla (1976, completed 1981), by Enrique Perea and Gabriel Ruíz Cabrera. Set on an awkward corner, where building restrictions required four storeys on one side and six on the other, the site demanded a fresh approach. The essential Andalucian patio, providing shade and circulation of cool air in the hot summers, is placed behind a false façade, which also forms the formal entrance. This building and the Bankinter were the first examples of a new kind of

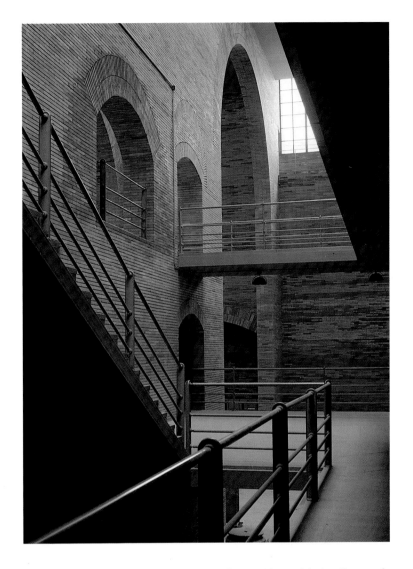

OPPOSITE *The Banco de Bilbao by Francisco Javier Saenz de Oiza, 1971. One of the old masters of architecture, de Oiza was the teacher and mentor of Rafael Moneo, who in turn has strongly influenced the work of Alberto Campo Baeza, one of Madrid's foremost architects today.*

El Museo Nacional de Arte Romano de Mérida, by Rafael Moneo, 1985. Three-storey high Roman arches are built entirely of brick, devoid of any decoration apart from brickwork patterning. Metal walkways break through the supporting walls. The Mérida Museum symbolizes another great architectonic change in Spain, with its boldness and lack of frivolity.

29

La Casa Olerdola by Jaume Bach and Gabriel Mora, 1981. Here the architects have challenged conventions such as the boundary between outside and inside, and even the habitual privacy of the bathroom. The sparse bathroom and indoor pool are separated by only a glass wall; the pool can open onto a terrace which can be covered to provide an additional outdoor room.

architecture sometimes known as eclectic rationalism, which owes little to Modernism, instead respecting traditional necessities and regional context while presenting a moderate and simplistic solution.

PRIVATE HOUSES

In Barcelona, the firm Estudio Per (Oscar Tusquets Blanca, Lluís Clotet, Pep Bonet and Cristian Cirici) was extremely active at this time. Tusquets is typically Catalan, loving to challenge, question and break the rules. He insists that his architectural training taught him nothing, and that he only began to learn when working for a former teacher he admired, Federico Correa. He knows that his work is seen by Madrid and Sevillian architects as decorative and mannered, as is his love of detail, but rationalism and Modernism bore him. The more historical reference he can allude to in his work, the happier he is, and he uses rich materials combined with traditional techniques to ensure that his work will grow old gracefully.

The leisure-loving Spanish lifestyle gives rise to many and varied private commissions. In 1975 Tusquets and Clotet had built the highly imaginative Casa en la Isla de Pantellería, a private house on an island off Italy. Tucked into a hillside above the sea, it has wide terraces with Neoclassical pillars, which are free-standing and can support cane matting to provide shade in summer. The interior is also heavily based on Roman villas, with sunken baths and a sparse but light atmosphere.

A sunken bath in an airy bathroom separated from an indoor pool by only a glass wall is a feature of the little Casa Olerdola, built in Barcelona in 1981 by Jaume Bach and Gabriel Mora. A massive canvas awning

ARCHITECTURE

covers the wide marble terrace and a large portion of the garden. The Casa Boenders on Ibiza, built in 1979/83 by Elías Torres and José Antonio Martínez Lapena, has a large L-shaped pool taking up most of one of a series of terraces, whose other features are truncated pillars and stone or brick stairways.

Winner of one of the prestigious FAD (Fomento de las Artes Decorativas) Architecture prizes for 1988 is the imaginative Casa Gay by Antoní de Moragas and Irene Sánchez-Hernando. Set on a hill above Barcelona, this three-storey house has both open and covered decks and terraces inside and a steeply terraced garden and pool. The use of untreated and polished wood, weatherboarding and decking give the house a rural aspect, and a massive rock outcrop incorporated into a wall in a starkly modern living area combine to produce a home that is resonant with memories of Alvar Aalto's Villa Mairea.

Alfredo Arribas, a young lion of Barcelona, especially well-known for his interiors of fashionable night spots, has produced a little jewel of a house, tucked in between two old buildings on a Barcelona street. The interior of the Casa Pastor building has been completely reorganized, with an additional floor and roof terrace added. A special feature of the house is the use Arribas and his collaborator Miguel Morte have made of patios and light wells to add height and natural light to a space which, apart from its street façade, is entirely enclosed. The ceiling heights are varied – the main bathroom on the first floor, for example, is double height, reaching natural light. It also houses an alternative access to the second floor, via a staircase whose treads are cantilevered out from the

LEFT *The living area of the Casa Pastor residence in Barcelona, with exterior refurbishment and complete interior reconstruction by Alfredo Arribas and Miguel Morte, 1985/87. The walnut panelled shelving and marble fireplace provide a homely focal point for the house, which is otherwise very bright and cool, with open-plan room arrangements. Photo by Jordi Sarrá.*

Stairway to the new roof terrace and added floor of Alfredo Arribas and Miguel Morte's Casa Pastor residence. The sensuously curving iron handrail and dainty balustrade soften the effect of harsh white walls. The skylight high above the stairs has screens of variable depth suspended from it, filtering the otherwise blinding sunlight. Photo by Jordi Sarrá.

ARCHITECTURE

wall. Interior spaces are arranged to give views through arches and doorways, each of which have different light sources; mirrors also confuse the sense of perspective and give extra depth. Glazed garage doors at street level include a monogram designed by Arribas, and the façade rises to a double height arch shielding the new floor and roof terrace.

Jordi Garcés and Enric Soría use Minimalist principles in their work, but without the large scale or the high technology which are the everyday tools of many architects of this school. They prefer more common materials which have a richer texture. Oriol Bohigas, in his introduction to the monograph *Garcés/Soría* (Gustavo Gili, 1987), says that because of this, 'it is possible to interpret comprehensively the work of these architects within the Reductionist tradition of Modern Art, which springs from Dada and which has been present in many, and certainly the most fruitful, variations of Modernism . . . the architecture of this century has always had an intimate connection with this series of Reductionisms, and not only in the more immediate reference to Minimalism. Garcés and Soría . . . are a good example of how slight an influence the writing and work of [Robert] Venturi and his followers have had in Catalonia.' Their design for the Casa G Hidalgo in Allela, Barcelona, completed in 1987, is set in the hills with spectacular views reflected in the mirrored windows of a series of white cubes set on a wide irregular terrace.

A triangular house with a car park on the second floor may not sound appealing, but was the only practical solution to building on an awkwardly shaped site plunging down the hills of Barcelona. It was in 1988 that the architect Carlos Ferrater produced this magnificent dwelling, called by *ARDI* magazine *La cascada de cristal* (glass waterfall) because of its four falls of glass on the south façade, one for each floor. An imposing double height entrance hall is flanked by car parking space, above which is a sitting room in the eaves of the house. Below are a floor of bedrooms and a floor of living space, which gives on to terraced gardens with pergolas, benches and solariums, leaving no corner of this compact site to chance.

Even more extraordinary is the Casa Turegano by Alberto Campo Baeza of Madrid. Campo is a major figure in the Madrid architectural scene, and a group of younger architects has formed around him. A teacher, theorist and writer on architecture, he describes himself as 'a thinker who built . . . a builder who thought'. The Casa Turegano, built in 1988, and another example of siting on a hillside outside the city to

Built as a series of cubes on a wide terrace, the Casa Hidalgo by Jordi Garcés and Enric Soría (1987), is set in the hills of Allela outside Barcelona. Using the idiom of Minimalist architecture but on a smaller, domestic scale, the work of these architects falls within the Reductionist tradition, using low-tech materials and traditional techniques on highly sophisticated designs.

OPPOSITE *A corner of the stunning Casa Turegano by Alberto Campo Baeza, 1988, what he calls his 'white and cubical hut', set on a terraced plot outside Madrid. A perfect cube punctured only by occasional large glazed areas, the three-storey house plays on room dimensions inside, with double and triple ceiling heights alternating like a Chinese puzzle.*

34

ARCHITECTURE

capture any breezes, is for him the realization of a dream. Campo calls this economical 'tense cubic building' his 'white and cubical hut'. There are three floors, with the entrance by the middle level. The layout has bedrooms upstairs and sitting room downstairs, with two double height spaces overlapping to give complete penetration by natural light of the entire building.

PUBLIC BUILDINGS

To an outsider, one of the most inspiring aspects of Spanish architecture is the amount of public money spent on really fine buildings – schools, nurseries, colleges, museums, public housing and institutions, sports stadiums and hospitals. The new regional autonomous authorities have had generous funds put at their disposal to refurbish town halls, administrative offices and other public buildings. Barcelona in particular has benefited retrospectively from Franco's distrust of the Catalan nation: funds for the upkeep and rebuilding of the city had been frozen for years, but have now been released with accumulated interest, facilitating some very ambitious schemes. New public buildings, once erected, are maintained to a very high standard: many have full-time cleaning staff constantly on hand to sweep floors and empty ashtrays; flooring is polished and brass buffed to within an inch of its life.

Alberto Campo Baeza was commissioned in 1985 to build an extension to the existing school of San Fermín in Madrid. His three-storey, long narrow building is of the simplest design with corridors to the north and classrooms to the south. But the entrance to the building is a massive cylinder, projecting through either wall, with an outer surface composed almost entirely of glass bricks. The main staircase is set into this structure, providing a lovely, airy luminous space for this unofficial meeting place. Campo also completed, in partnership with Javier Esteban Martín, no less than three nursery schools in 1982 alone. His language of clean white spaces with lots of natural light is particularly suited to buildings of this kind.

The architecture of Portaceli, sometimes called neo-Modern as it seems torn between Classicism and Modernism, has links to that of Campo. His school – the Escuela Gravina at Picanya in Valencia, finished in 1984 – is almost monumental, with massive cliff-like white walls reminiscent of Mies van der Rohe at his most radical.

On a more modest scale, the school designed in Barcelona by Jordi Bosch, Joan Tarrus and Santí Vives in 1985 addressed the problem of a corner site in the centre of the city. An uncompromising wedge-shaped building projects out of the corner, while additional outdoor space is provided by a wide open corridor with artificial window spaces and a covered walkway four storeys above the Barcelona traffic.

Probably the best known new railway station is also in Barcelona. It is that of Estación Sants, built by Helio Piñon and Alberto Viaplana in 1984. It has a vast paved piazza with an eccentric walkway sheltered from the

Alberto Campo Baeza's school at San Fermín, built in 1985. A long rectangular building with a corridor running the length of one side, otherwise virtually featureless, is imaginatively relieved by a massive cylindrical tower which projects from either side of the building, and holds the staircase. Imaginative use of the humble glass brick has transformed it into something spectacular. Photo by Paco Rojo.

ARCHITECTURE

Bellaterra Station, which serves a Barcelona university, by Jaume Bach and Gabriel Mora, 1984. This small neo-Modernist structure is one of a number of architect-designed railway stations around Spain.

Mediterranean sun. Abstract, but with a distinctly organic sculptural form, Sants accepts the technology which holds the building up, while at the same time acknowledging both the necessities of life in a hot country and the eclectic tastes of its public. Bellaterra railway station, which serves the Barcelona university of that name, is a small-scale Neo-modernist structure, completed in 1984 by Jaume Bach and Gabriel Mora.

In strong contrast is one of Raphael Moneo's recent projects in Madrid, the conversion of Atocha railway station into an exhibition and conference centre. This, begun in 1988, has a huge and magnificent leaded arch window and iron girder-braced barrel roof. Set across the end of the Paseo de la Castellana, almost within sight of his early masterpiece, the Bankinter, it involved shifting an entire terminus. It will be completed in good time for Madrid's Cultural Capital of the Year celebrations in 1992.

In the early '70s, Taller de Arquitectura, the studio of Ricardo Bofill, was beginning to make its mark with experimental work. Bofill was one of the first truly adventurous Spanish architects, and his spirit – though not his style – has influenced the new generation. Bofill himself is now a true post-Modernist, constantly referring to Classical motives, but manipulating them to his needs. His style has little relation to Spanish culture, transcending rather than assimilating regional themes. Examples of his most enduring work, built in the early '70s, are found around Calpe, near Alicante, in various apartment blocks overlooking the sea. He combined Neoclassical and monumental forms, bravely articulated, while using the latest technology. This satisfied human needs while at the same time exploring the role of architecture, and served as a forerunner of the pioneering post-Modern role which Bofill came to play on the international scene.

But this is a very mature post-Modernism, bearing little relationship to the easily imitated 'children's building block' style which many adopted. When Bofill was commissioned by the Communist local authority at Marne-la-Vallée near Paris to create a large public housing complex (1974, completed 1980), he produced a confident masterpiece. It consists of massive forms, unashamedly Neoclassic, with pillars rising nine storeys, archways punched through the blocks, topped with pediments and friezes with French Classical references. The complex has the shape of a closed U, with a nine-storey triumphal arch across the middle which also contains apartments. Constructed totally in prefabricated sections, it is technically as well as aesthetically revolutionary.

Spanish autonomous authorities have also proved to be very adventurous clients. The 1988 FAD-award-winning public housing complex in Mollet del Valles, Catalonia, is the work of Josep Martorell, Oriol Bohigas and David Mackay, a group which, with Bohigas at its head, has been responsible for many of the city refurbishment schemes around Barcelona. Bohigas is seen by many as the 'tío' or uncle of Catalan architecture, and is the author of many books and articles on the subject. This particular complex of 200 apartments has a large paved courtyard in its centre, with plants and covered pathways. The very dignified buildings feature an open terrace of columns on the uppermost floor. The blocks are joined by a network of connecting walkways and stairways, which have both practical and social functions.

Another major housing block in Barcelona, built in the same year, is by Jordi Bosch, Joan Tarrus and Santí Vives. From the street is appears as a large cube solidly set on the ground, but it is in fact two sections joined by arches and stairways. The exterior is unmistakably post-Modern and is richly decorated with bowed balconies, extensive use of imaginative brickwork, and both tall and broad arches.

The Basque architect José Ignacio Linazasoro has likewise produced a post-Modern housing block in a city setting, but in a very different context. This five-storey building is in the old quarter of Vergara,

The fairytale or science fiction proportions of Taller de Arquitectura and Ricardo Bofill's public housing project at Marne la Vallée outside Paris (1974/80). Innumerable historical and classical references have been used in what was an advanced technology project, constructed entirely from prefabricated sections. This is Le Palacio of Les Espaces d'Abraxas, as the complex is called.

Ricardo Bofill's public housing complex at Marne la Vallée outside Paris, 1974-80. Le Théâtre D'Abraxas has nine-storey columns and French classical motives, the essence of post-Modernism commissioned by the communist local authority. This flight of fantasy was constructed entirely with prefabricated sections.

RIGHT Ricardo Bofill's dramatic Parc de la Marca Hispánica, 1978, a monument which allowed Bofill's imagination its full rein. Truncated columns, pavilions and Hollywood-style steps cover a mountainside.

41

ARCHITECTURE

Perspective of the new traffic and pedestrian areas at the Puerta del Sol in the heart of Madrid by Antón Capitel, 1984/86. With traffic concentrated down a single carriageway, and very broad pedestrian areas, this busy thoroughfare is also a centre of great social activity, venue for the evening paseo around the shops and cafes. The fountain seats have become a popular meeting place.

Guipúzcoa, and is placed between two existing palaces. Built on a similar scale to its neighbours, it has a pantiled roof, decorative brickwork and iron window grilles. Its most imposing features are a row of plaster festoons between the upper windows and a cylindrical entrance lobby the height of the building.

OPEN SPACES

Bofill's extraordinary Parc de la Marca Hispanica of 1978, a monument situated in a park in the mountains near the French border, is perhaps a symbol of the extent of imagination that was used in the design of public spaces throughout the '80s. With breath-defying steps reaching to the sky, seas of truncated columns and heroic pavilions, it is a combination of Hollywood, ancient Greece and Aztec Peru – a characteristic piece of theatre from this flamboyant architect.

The complete reorganization and restoration of one of Madrid's major thoroughfares and bus termini, La Puerta del Sol, was undertaken by Antón Capitel and his partners Antonio Riviere and Javier Ortega in 1984/6. The original square, with two fountains on a long central grassed reserve, was a disaster both aesthetically and practically, since it hindered the flow of traffic. Moving the space to one side to form an extremely wide area encompassing the fountains has not only had the effect of funnelling the traffic more directly across the square, but has also provided a focal point for the evening social activities which are so much a part of Spanish life. The fountains, surrounded by circular seating areas, have become the place to rendezvous with friends. Monumental street lights, whose classical allusions complement the fine buildings around the square, are an unusual feature, as are the column-shaped low-level lights dotted at frequent intervals along the pavements. All the details of the square, such as kiosks, phone booths, signposts and bus-stops, have also been standardized, and, as a final flourish, all the original façades of golden stone have been restored.

Beth Galí has several public parks to her name, two of which are Joan Miró Park and Fossar de la Pedrera, both in Barcelona. She was selected for the restricted competition for the Parc de Bercy in Paris, and won first prize in the international competition for the Parc de la Villette in 1983. Now in command of Barcelona's urban regeneration programme, she both designs and commissions for this vast and complex project, while continuing to stimulate her imagination with alternative projects: so far these have included a number of theatrical productions as well as fashion shows.

A sense of tradition is clearly expressed in Oscar Tusquet's and Lluís Clotet's Casa en la Isla de Pantelleria (see page 31) of 1975. Deliberately evoking a Roman ruin, the villa has a series of patios and terraces which fall down the hillside.

Perhaps echoing the curvaceous seating of Gaudí's Parc Güell, the seating in the Plaza Mayor de Parets del Valles, Barcelona, forms angles which produce different conversational groups. Enric Miralles and Carmen Pinos designed a complex cross-over of benches and sunshades which form a delightfully haphazard pattern across a compact space. Galí's plans for Barcelona incorporate innumerable new squares, either tucked into disused land or in the major new development for the Olympic village by the sea. All are furnished with shady walkways, fountains, drinking-water taps and creative new forms of lighting, some bordering on sculpture.

CONVERSION AND RESTORATION

The presence of so many fine ancient buildings is one of the most important assets of Spanish architecture, and their solidity and permanence are qualities many architects strive for – and often achieve. Many old buildings have been converted successfully to serve institutional or administrative purposes, while the National Paradors, the network of government-run hotels all over the country, are set in converted castles, palaces, convents and monasteries. Other marvellous ancient buildings have now become art galleries or museums.

The Catholic religious tradition in Spain, though slowly dwindling, is still strong, and many religious orders are very wealthy. This means that modern restoration or expansion work of religious buildings is common, with the clients more open to adventurousness than one might expect. So the tradition of the Church as patron of the arts continues. Many precious ancient churches, convents and monasteries were vandalized during the Civil War and have been restored. One which had been left abandoned for years is El Recinto de la Cartuja, a religious retreat on an island in the river at Seville. El Recinto is now to be the centre of the massive development for the World Expo '92 (see Chapter 7). Some convents and monasteries which have outgrown their usefulness have either been sold or thoughtfully converted by their former occupants into peaceful residences or elegant museums. Some have magnificent secluded gardens which transform well to new uses.

The Convento de las Beates in Gerona was converted into apartments and offices by Josep Fuses and Josep María Viader in 1985. Built into a hillside, the historic convent is a very tall, U-shaped building, whose modern additions do not impinge too harshly on the original building. The Iglesia de Nuestra Señora de Montserrat in Madrid was never finished, leaving a rough west wall behind the main altar. Antón Capitel was asked to add a presbytery and sacristy, also adding a new high altar. The result, completed in 1985 after three years' work, was a new wing in keeping with the old church but adhering to Capitel's philosophy of 'combining tradition with modernity'. The small town of Medina de Rioseca in Valladolid is the home of a once-magnificent church, Santa Cruz, of which only the outer walls, tower and façade remained. The

The new wing of the church of
Nuestra Señora de Montserrat,
Madrid, by Antón Capitel, 1985.
Though it was in need of restoration,
the original church had never been
finished. Now with a presbytery and
sacristy, the very simple
Hoffmanesque motives of his new
addition blend favourably with the
lines of the restored earlier church.

ARCHITECTURE

roof and interior were completely ruined through disuse and decay. José Ignacio Linazasoro had to reconstruct the nave walls, wooden vaulted ceiling and roof across a void of 19 metres (69 feet), a feat which he accomplished (1985/8) in a style which blends successfully with that of the original building, using historical analogy rather than imitation or pastiche. The glued wooden vault is particularly spectacular, reaching up to an elliptically shaped cupola above the main altar. Decorative detail is kept to a minimum, allowing original features to take precedence.

A highly imaginative conversion of a group of abandoned buildings transformed L'Hort de les Monges (the Nuns' Orchard) at Cabrils into a bar and restaurant. Alfredo Arribas, the designer of uncompromisingly modern bars in Barcelona, found an unusual solution to the problem set by a labyrinth of buildings, stairways, walkways and different levels, which needed a focal point to combine them. His three-storey tower, replica of a medieval one, which sits in the middle of the group, is built with traditional techniques and materials, almost defying you to call it new. A typical Catalan spiral staircase with no central support curls up one wall. All decorations and furnishings are deliberately antiqued, to confuse still further the differentiation between the old and the new.

The Centro de Arte Reina Sofía in Madrid was created to provide the first permanent centre for the cultural and artistic life of the country. Set near both the Museo del Prado and the Biblioteca Nacional, its ideology is also between the two – it is both an exhibition centre and one for learning, discussion and debate. It was originally a massive hospital built in the late eighteenth century by Sabatini to the designs of Hermosillo, six floors high and centring on a huge quadrangle. Until 1965 it housed the Madrid Provincial Hospital, but when this was relocated the building came under the threat of partial demolition. However, moves were made in 1969 to have it listed as a historic building, and it finally acquired this status soon after the State acquired it in 1976.

Having decided on the building's new role, general restoration work was begun in 1980 by architect Antonio Fernández Alba. Competitions for restoration and conversion of the interior were held, with top architects from all regions of Spain being commissioned for each area of the museum (see Chapter 2 for full descriptions of the interiors). The first phase was opened to the public in 1986.

Perhaps the strangest reconstruction is that of the famous Mies van der Rohe Pavilion in Montjuïc Park, Barcelona, the summation of Modernism, originally built as the German pavilion for the World Fair in 1929. Years of neglect necessitated its subsequent removal, and it was totally rebuilt by Ignacio Solá-Morales, Francisco Ramos and Cristian Cirici in 1986, as an act of homage to the great man. Situated close to the stadium at the heart of the main Olympic complex, it is a great attraction for those on design pilgrimages to Barcelona.

OPPOSITE *Interior from the reconstruction of the Mies van der Rohe pavilion on its original site by Ignacio Solá-Morales, Francisco Ramos and Cristian Cirici (1986). The original building was the German pavilion for the 1929 Barcelona International Exhibition.*

Interior of the newly built 'medieval' tower at the restaurant of L'Hort de les Monges (nun's orchard) outside Barcelona, by Alfredo Arribas and Miguel Morte, 1986/7. The deepset window and doorway light the typical Catalan spiral staircase. Photo by Jordi Sarrá.

47

ARCHITECTURE

LEFT *The lower floor of the Museo Picasso extension in the Meca Palace, Barcelona, refurbished by Jordi Garcés and Enric Soría. The architectonic qualities of the room are emphasized by the lighting of bricked vaults, while tile patterning deceives the eye. Many areas are left deliberately unrestored.*

RIGHT *Uncompromisingly modern, the new entrance and lobby to a nineteenth-century former lunatic asylum, converted in 1979 to become Barcelona's Science Museum by Jordi Garcés and Enric Soría.*

MUSEUMS AND CONCERT HALLS

The team of Jordi Garcés and Enric Soría are responsible for extensions to two of the best known museums in Barcelona. The conversion of a quasi-Modernist asylum by Domènech i Estapa into a science museum in 1979 illustrates their reductionist principles. The addition, making only the most basic and minimal references to the existing building, is purposely modern, with no decoration to complement the earlier highly detailed façade. The refurbishment of the Meca Palace as an extension to the Picasso Museum is more easily understood. As Oriol Bohigas explains: 'It allows the old building to express itself with all its wounds and mutilations, magnifies its decay and adds only a few exact gestures . . . The patching in place of restoration, the doors left still almost disintegrating, the cracks, the remnants of the old Baroque and Neo-classical decoration, the respect for the incomplete, make up a surprising composition . . .'.

Probably the best known of Spain's new museums, which the public and international critics alike have hailed as a great success, is Rafael Moneo's Museo Nacional de Arte Romano (1985), in Merida, Badajoz. The Merida museum is an architectural landmark, showing the Spanish architects' compromise between tradition and modernity at its strongest, and evidencing their refusal to take any style to extremes. The imposing interior has a series of three-storey-high Roman arches, entirely built of brick. Metal walkways are punched through the supporting walls –

ambulatories rather than simply means of transport. The only decoration is simple fan shapes in brickwork above the arches. Massive skylights give soft natural light over this authoritative and calmly atmospheric building.

When Valencia's main river began its gradual process of drying out, small boys used the riverbed as a football pitch, and this natural amenity, a long, centrally placed open space, has now been properly reclaimed for use by the city. Parks, gardens – and paved football pitches – have been installed. A garden, including water gardens, has been designed by Ricardo Bofill. Part of this complex is an incomparable concert hall built by the great Sevillian architect, José María García de Paredes. El Palau de la Musica (the Music Palace) opened in late 1987, and world-standard conductors and musicians have testified that it has the best, or among the best, acoustic qualities of all concert halls in Europe.

The huge lobby of this T-shaped building is composed of three shells. The outer one is like a giant white portico, with a row of simple square pillars which are reflected in what is left of the River Turia. The middle shell is a rounded oblong structure, entirely glassed, which gives a golden glow at night, reminiscent of Joseph Paxton's nineteenth-century masterpiece in England, the Crystal Palace. The inner shell comprises the stairways and galleries necessary to reach the various parts of the three auditoriums, which are all sited in the descender of the T.

This startling building, designed for popular use by one of Spain's great architects who, although approaching his seventies, uses the latest technology, stands as a symbol of contemporary Spanish architecture.

50

INTERIOR DESIGN

'We should stop pretending that everything is invented; it clearly isn't. Whoever says they don't copy is an innocent or a liar. To design is to manipulate. It is not to invent forms but rather to put existing ones together, as this is how they are transformed.'

(ALFREDO ARRIBAS, ARDI MAGAZINE, MARCH/APRIL 1988)

Gaudí's Stone Quarry building photographed at dusk on the Paseo de la Castellana. The top floor apartment belongs to Fernando Amat, founder of Barcelona's prime design shop, Vincon. The interior design and most of the furniture are by Carlos Riart.

The first visible sign of the coming of age of a country in design terms is the infiltration of fashion and fashion awareness among ordinary people; the second is a proliferation of interior design. This area can be as transient and as expendable as fashion; indeed the two are often interconnected, with shops, bars and restaurants owned by or frequented by those who lead and feed the world of fashion.

But, to the Spanish nature, culture and the enjoyment of culture in its various forms are as essential as eating well and enjoying congenial company in sympathetic surroundings, and there are less hard and fast divisions between one area of design and another. The people responsible for the design of a fashionable shop or bar might also take on the refurbishment of a museum or the installation of a fine-art exhibition at a prestigious venue. Likewise, the team responsible for revitalizing an urban centre, deciding where to move the sewage works, taking into account traffic circulation and placing bus stops, might also design the stage and costumes for an avant-garde theatrical performance.

Most commercial interior design in Spain is executed by architects. The word *interiorista*, while sometimes describing interior designers, is also used for interior decorators and has derogatory overtones not appreciated by the main body of the profession. The most commonly used term is 'interior architect', a definition that reveals something about the Spanish attitude to interior design. It is seen as something permanent and lasting, at any rate more so than the type of retail and commercial design so prevalent in the UK throughout the '80s, which had a life expectancy of around 18 months. While the USA and the rest of Europe are now moving towards using better materials and more classic designs, Spain has always designed in this way, thus largely avoiding the hectic mid-'80s design boom which devoured so many ideas – and careers – in so short a space of time.

THE CENTRO DE ARTE

By far the largest and most ambitious interior design project in recent years has been the refurbishment of the Centro de Arte Reina Sofía in Madrid. With the active patronage of Queen Sofía, this conversion of a massive eighteenth-century hospital is intended to provide the country with a major centre for the acquisition, exhibition, discussion and diffusion of modern art. Classical art is well provided for, with museums and centres of learning all over Spain, but modern art has been less well served. A large part of twentieth-century Spanish art was produced outside the country by the many exiles driven out by the rigours of Franco's rule and his personal taste for figurative art. Pablo Picasso, Juan Gris and Joan Miró are probably the best known self-exiled painters, but many others in all areas of the arts found sanctuary abroad, most particularly in Paris. This has caused a yawning gap in the modern art history of the country. Even in the early '80s, when La Movida and the New Figurationist artists were causing a stir in the international art world, in Spain modern art remained the poor relation, surviving mainly on handouts or patronage from private sources. The '90s look more promising on this front, with the regional autonomies becoming more determined to nurture this important side of their local culture.

The Centre is intended to play an active part in the development of Spanish modern art; its remit is to be a focus of artistic and cultural debate for the entire country and all of its autonomous regions. Although this is a very worthy aim for an art centre based in a capital city, and provides an opportunity for thousands of overseas visitors to gain an overall view of Spanish art, many of the autonomies are hostile to this aspect of the centre's function. The prospect of the removal of many of the finest works of art in their possession, which could strip them of the best of their own cultural attractions, has caused a great deal of friction with Madrid.

The wide-ranging responsibilities of the Centre have been catered for by the provision of different areas. The Twentieth Century Art Galleries house permanent collections as well as holding temporary exhibitions. The Design Department includes product design – encompassing fashion, consumer goods and artisan products as well as industrial (and communication) design – signing, editorial design, posters and corporate identity. The Department of Image is responsible for photography, cinema, video and other visual media. The Documentation Centre includes a library of books, magazines, music, video, photography and slides, and has set up a database whose eventual scope should be very broad. The Department of Communication is responsible for internal as well as external diffusion of information. A Department of Contemporary Music completes this highly ambitious project.

In 1986 the first phase of the refurbishment was set in motion, put into the hands of André Ricard, a well established designer of the older generation who practises in many different disciplines. He was to select designers for each area of the project, from different parts of Spain,

One of the sculpture galleries at the Centro de Arte Reina Sofía by Juan Ariño Bayón, 1986/7. Windows set in walls 2 metres thick softly light the high vaults. Galleries on the floor below have even higher ceilings. The great length of the rooms gives a rare perspective to larger pieces of work. Photo by Tom Frankland.

INTERIOR DESIGN

though for some reason this did not prove to be possible. General restoration work on the fabric and façade of the building, including its remarkable stone stairways, was executed by Antonio Fernández Alba. His main concern was to remove any late additions to the building which were considered unsympathetic to its original plan, and to restore any damaged parts of the exterior as accurately as possible and with identical materials. The interior layout was also to be restored to its original condition, the only adaptation allowed being to accommodate wiring and other technological requirements where necessary.

The first area you enter of the Centro de Arte Reina Sofía is the lobby, with adjoining information desk, gift shop and bookshop. The team of Elias Torres and José Antonio Martínez Lapena was chosen to give a distinctive look to the five rooms to the right of the entrance, which is in the centre of the main façade. They decided to create a structure which would join, visually and physically, all the rooms, while providing the various necessities such as showcases, desks, counters and screens. It was important not to detract from the magnificent structure of the rooms, which have original brickwork right up to the top of the vaulted ceilings. Made up of a series of triangles, the installation forms a canopy like a spider's web attached to different points of each room, beneath which the fittings and pieces of furniture sit.

The café and restaurant, on the ground floor and in the basement

The 1986 design by Elias Torres and José Martínez Lapeña for the entrance lobby and information desk of the Centro de Arte Reina Sofía. A very light spidersweb construction spans the room without detracting from its own magnificent proportions. Photo by Tom Frankland.

respectively, were also completed in 1986; they were designed by Federico Correa and Alfonso Milá, both in their sixties and from Barcelona. The restaurant has a barrel-vaulted ceiling, like nearly all of the rooms, with no proper windows but with deep-set diagonal skylights from street level. The café has large windows onto the street. Both areas have been floored with black and white marble tiles with all brickwork plastered and painted white. Large mirrors, varnished wood panelling, huge fringed ceiling lamps and Thonet chairs give a curious and very sober turn-of-the-century atmosphere.

The press room, protocol rooms and first-aid room are the work of the well-established interior and industrial designer, Miguel Milá. The colour theme is very simple and calm, with a reassuring grey used for walls, furniture and fittings, offset by white marble floors. Extra long, low, rectangular, grey leather sofas were specially designed. The protocol rooms are on two levels with a gallery, joined by a spiral staircase.

Jaume Bach and Gabriel Mora were chosen to create the lecture hall. One square and one long room divided by a central arch provided an obvious lobby and hall, with frequent large windows down one side. It was very important throughout this project to interfere as little as possible with the structure, and to incorporate the many technological services of such a room with the minimum of structural or visual interference. To improve the acoustics, a triangular structure has been built at the entrance to the hall; acoustic boxes partly block the windows, and a triangular canopy, which also supports the projector and video camera, hangs over the podium. The seating area is inclined, to improve both visual and auditory qualities. Decoration has been kept very simple,

Another view of the original lobby design by Elias Torres and José Martínez Lapeña, this one showing the gift shop and display area. Tall arches and exposed brickwork vaulting can clearly be seen. Photo by Tom Frankland.

INTERIOR DESIGN

Centro de Arte Reina Sofía: entrance to the fine art galleries by Juan Ariño Bayón. This shows the granite doorjambs which were considered possibly to interfere with the 'silence' of the spaces. Photo by Tom Frankland.

with the only hint of frivolity being a Neo-classical clouded sky painted on the vault.

The refurbishment of the exhibition rooms must be one of the most masterly accomplishments of the Centre. These, by Madrileño Juan Ariño Bayon, do not appear to have been touched by the hand of a designer. But this was exactly his intention – to create the most neutral possible surroundings for these spaces where so many highly varied exhibits are to be seen. Each of the four sides of the building has two galleries running parallel, with double-vaulted ceilings joined by deep window openings and doorways along the centre. The original layout is almost perfect for transformation to its new uses, with very little interference necessary. This is fortunate, as many of the walls are up to two metres (six feet) thick.

Ariño Bayon decided to remove from the rooms any details which might attract the attention of visitors, leaving them almost severely plain. There was great discussion at one time about whether the granite door jambs, contrasting with the rough marble floor tiles, interfered with the 'spatial silence' of the galleries. White-painted walls and ceilings, very subtle artificial lighting, and the magnificent natural light flooding in from the high windows set deep into the thick walls and diffused by the vaulted ceilings, are the only decoration deemed suitable.

The top floor or attic space is devoted to the Contemporary Music Centre and Department of Image. Much of the high triangular roof space (with skylights) is unsuitable for use by the public, and is used for storage and study purposes, with long shelving units down each side holding all kinds of documents and material. The architects Javier Feduchi and Javier Velles have formed a regular series of square units along the middle of the space to be used as study areas or simply as skylit patios. The main wing of the building has a much larger attic, and here a public space has been created for exhibitions, concerts and recitals of contemporary music.

André Ricard is responsible also for the refurbishment of the long corridors and the public lavatories. Specially designed ceiling lights, some giving soft uplighting to emphasize the vaults and others a brighter downlighting, have a classic appearance which does not compete with the architectonic qualities of archways, ceilings and windows along the corridors. Set at regular intervals, the uniformity of the lights appears to increase the corridors' length. The benches, ashtrays and rubbish bins have been set into the narrow recesses between the pilasters, reinforcing the sense of uncluttered perspective and also keeping these essential items out of the way of visitors. Ricard's lavatories, devised first for the press rooms and subsequently installed all around the building, are equally impressive. His first concern was for their use and maintenance, as he believes that not only their quality but also their appearance in the middle of a busy day are an important factor in the visitors' overall perception of a public building. The simplest fittings – simple in construction and simple to use – have been chosen, and the most economical use has been made of the most robust materials, which will

Centro de Arte Reina Sofía: the refurbishment of the corridors was by André Ricard, who was also in overall charge of the original scheme. Here, ground-floor corridors have series of windows in arched recesses giving onto the garden. Ricard's pendant lights stretch the great length of this impressive void. Photo by Tom Frankland.

INTERIOR DESIGN

The ground and first floor of Otto Zutz nightclub, Barcelona, by Alicia Nuñez and Guillem Bonet. The first floor is very spacious with a pool table; a gallery at second floor height ends the deep well, which has the dance-floor at the bottom. Photo by Jordi Sarrá.

clean easily. The walls and floors are granite, all the sanitary fittings stainless steel, while the false ceilings inside are lacquered aluminium. All these appear to meet Ricard's strict requirements, both hygienically and aesthetically.

DESIGNER BARS

No overview of interiors in Spain would be complete without reference to the many and diverse fashionable bars of Madrid and Barcelona. There are many very ancient bars with centuries-old traditions which have barely been touched by the passing of time – except that they now sell light beer. And there are many beautiful relics from the last century, with Art Nouveau tiling, panelling, fittings and furniture, which are unlikely ever to change. But the range, in age and social status, of people who frequent cafés, restaurants and tapas bars, passing from one to the next to sample their specialities, has broadened, and the market has naturally answered their needs.

The reasons for the proliferation of designer bars were explained by Juli Capella, co-editor of the Barcelona magazine *ARDI*, in his address to the ICSID/Design 87 conference in Amsterdam, 'Drink and Design'. The first was the continuation of ancient traditions; the second the number of young impresarios wanting to renovate interesting venues; and the third the large number of high-quality designers with a personal approach to their work. The architect Oriol Bohigas wrote in an article for the Italian magazine *Abitare* that 'these interiors go way beyond the ordinary rules of architectural composition ... they express the exuberance and dynamism of the nightlife of the young population of Barcelona'. Many of them, he said, make 'ironic use of certain conventional forms and exaggeration in the direction of Modern or pre-Modern, even extra-Modern, recalling the '40s and '50s ... a décor that is aggressively trendy or that plays to the gratuitous excesses of the young clientele'. While these interiors may be more transitory than others mentioned here, they are no less important.

One of the earliest Barcelona bars is Zig Zag, designed in 1980 and overhauled in 1983. The décor has very distinctive '50s Hollywood references, such as massive doorways and chromed streamlining, but all deliberately cold and hard, in a style which was called *onda fría* (cold wave). The architects were Alicia Nuñez and Guillem Bonet, who also designed Otto Zutz in 1985, with the graphic designers Pati Nuñez and Alfonso Sostres. This is an especially interesting collaboration because all the participants are also part-owners of the club. Housed in a former warehouse with four floors, it has a complex arrangement of stairways with a large well down the centre leading to the ground-floor disco. Because lighting and colour effects can totally transform the appearance

Another spectacular staircase, this time at KGB bar by Alfredo Vidal, 1984. Set in a warehouse building, KGB's other outstanding feature is a moveable bar, to the left of the picture. Photo by Jordi Sarrá.

INTERIOR DESIGN

Network Bar and Restaurant, Barcelona, designs by Eduardo Samsó and Alfredo Arribas, 1987. MAIN PICTURE View of the circular well shows the striking combination of materials – metal flooring and beaten metal counters, wooden rails. TOP View of the wooden staircase, descending from the ground level entrance with its video wall.

ABOVE The Network logo by Pati Nuñez and Alfonso Sostres. The lower floors of the three-tier café are underground. Photos by Jordi Sarrá.

of the interior, this has been kept simple to act as a backdrop to the all-important social activities.

Alfredo Vidal's KGB, designed in 1984, is also a warehouse bar. Obvious spy themes are introduced in strip-cartoon-style posters, and the bar itself is placed on a platform like a train wagon so that it can be moved around at will. It is attached to services suspended from the ceiling. By contrast, Eduardo Samsó's Nick Havanna bar of 1986 leaves nothing to chance. Mixing his favourite styles of the Modern Movement with post-Modern influences, he created what was called at the time 'the ultimate bar'.

Samsó collaborated with Alfredo Arribas, of whom more later, to create probably the most luxuriously appointed nightspot in 1987 – the restaurant and bar called Network. Inspired by the cult films *Blade Runner* and *Brazil*, the interiors are a mixture of sophisticated technology – banks of videos – and neo-primitivism, especially in the use of rough-surfaced materials. Its three floors, all underground, are connected by a huge oval well. Network's lavatories, richly coloured and with translucent glass doors and mirrors circled by snake-like creatures, are a special delight. The design won a coveted FAD award in 1987.

A late Modernist stuccoed corner house in Barcelona, with later decorative additions, is the site of the Dos Torres (two towers) bar. In 1988 Pep Zazurca was commissioned to make some major alterations to enlarge it. This was his first one-man commission; his previous experience included a period working for the urban design department of the government of Catalonia. A new entrance was formed by the addition of a metal stairway to the first floor. A large glass canopy from the original structure was moved up a floor to make sense of this radical change, and a little circular corner balcony was converted into a large lamp. New metal balconies have Hoffmannesque motifs which have been repeated inside. A structural wall with openings across the middle of this floor created some problems, but Zazurca solved them by installing a circular bar in the middle, formed by four semi-circular sections, one on each interface. This has the added advantage of eliminating any 'dead' areas behind or beside the bar, which opens onto a wide paved terrace to the rear of the building. The decoration is in a style described by Oriol Bohigas as 'composite reductionist, towards a new interpretation of purism and Minimalism'.

Jordi Garcés and Enric Soría were responsible for the design in 1988 of the bar at the Colegio de Arquitectos in Barcelona, whose main features are the use of grey terrazzo and the arresting juxtaposition of a circular hole sliced out of the stair wall, a circular table and, attached to the opposite wall, a circular shape of the same size and made in the same material. Spain's many colleges of architecture have the natural advantage of the occupants' profession. Commissions for this kind of work are usually settled by competitions, with the winners being highly regarded both inside and outside the profession. The publicity surrounding the competitions and the eventual winners provides a powerful incentive to put a great deal of extra work into these projects.

An exhibition area cleverly slotted under the stairs transforms an otherwise unusable space, extending the bar at the Colegio de Arquitectos in Barcelona, by Jordi Garcés and Enric Soría, 1988. Grey terrazzo stairs and flooring are strengthened by the positioning of the hole in the stair wall, the terrazzo circle opposite, and the third component, the circular table, taking what could have been merely elegant into another, artistic dimension.

INTERIOR DESIGN

62

LEFT *Pep Zazurca's first floor interior for the Dos Torres bar, Barcelona, 1989. Gleaming wooden floors and a minimum of strategically placed furniture purposely accentuate the circular room centre; through the window the verdant roof terrace is visible.*

The Norman Foster-inspired entrance to the nightclub Velvet (Alfredo Arribas and Miguel Morte, 1988), which is themed on David Lynch's 1987 movie, Blue Velvet *(itself drawing heavily on the work of Luis Buñuel). Aluminium doors open onto two shapes covered with rough red velvet. Light pools spot the walkway and a palette shape – symbol of the club – is projected onto red velvet curtains. Photo by Jordi Sarrá.*

While a great majority of designer bars are in Barcelona, there are also many in Madrid, and other major cities are beginning to provide design-conscious night people with more exciting surroundings. Vitoria is the first city in the Basque Country to acquire one, in 1989, with the help of architects Roberto Ercilla and Miguel Ángel Campo. Called 4 Azules (four blues) it is largely decorated, as might be expected, in shades of blue. The long narrow space has a mysterious outer room leading into an atrium which houses the real entrance. An extraordinary metal stairway with no visible means of support leads to a spectacular metal walkway suspended above the bar which is used to reach services in the ceiling. The lower part of the ladder flips upwards to prevent its use by customers. A 9m (30ft) long white leather bench faces little round tables and blue lacquered chairs.

The bar stock is stored in an unusual way on metal shelves behind the bar at right angles to the bar counter, fitted with sliding wooden doors that can be drawn across them to conceal the interior completely. The lavatories are set behind a curving wall of translucent glass tiles, which glows with golden light at the back of the bar. Even the personnel are designed, bar staff being dressed by the fashion team of Luís Devota and Modesto Lomba.

ALFREDO ARRIBAS

For a long time the most fashionable bar in Barcelona has been Velvet, which opened in 1987. Inspired by the US film *Blue Velvet*, Alfredo Arribas and his regular collaborator Miguel Morte designed a modern Baroque bar, with many overlying references. There are two entrances to the very deep interior, one of which has a Norman Foster/Katherine Hamnett-inspired glass bridge. Polished rough-slate flooring and rough stone walls are juxtaposed defiantly with plush red velvet curtains, golden wood backgrounds and orange tiled pillars. The chairs and stools, with a design taken from a '50s original by Carlo Mollino, have oval split seats and backs reminiscent of carob nuts – or, disquietingly, of the human posterior. There is a circular teak dance floor in the middle of the room. The unisex lavatories have translucent walls and doors which do not encourage lingering – a recurrent device of Arribas'. Velvet presents a cacophony of styles which is not intended to be restful.

The same team was responsible for a larger, more ambitious project opened at the end of 1988 near Tarragona on a hillside overlooking the sea. This, called by *ARDI* magazine 'the Acropolis of leisure', is a complex of new buildings, gardens, terraces and pools, built on rocky waste

63

INTERIOR DESIGN

ground beside a railway line. It is entered over a bridge, with the first building containing entrance booths and cloakrooms. In a tribute to the US architect Frank Gehry, who was fond of including obscure features, a 'crashed' light aircraft projects tastelessly from an outside wall. A small tower holds the administrative offices. A complex arrangement of pathways, terraces and steps leads off towards the main disco building, which houses a video wall. One entire building or 'pavilion' houses the lavatories, and beside this is a large open terrace, partially covered, which looks towards the sea. Another bar, on two storeys, is totally enclosed, with one glass wall overlooking the garden and a waterfall which tumbles down to the swimming pool. The materials, furniture and fittings throughout the complex are all of the highest quality and have been chosen with great imagination, setting the seal on a highly imaginative project.

Arribas is at the height of his profession, and much in demand for fashionable work of this kind. One of his early projects was the interior for the Escuela Elisava design school in Barcelona, which was moved in 1986 into a semi-basement and basement. Studios, laboratories and class-rooms were needed, plus a large amount of storage space for archive material. Arribas chose a very calm and completely integrated style, with dark stained woods and polished stone floors. In order to create an illusion of space and height under the low ceilings, a long hall was fitted with a bank of cupboards reaching its entire length and inclining inwards from floor to ceiling. A rather eccentrically cut glass door increases the Alice in Wonderland effect. Translucent glass walls and a light metal staircase show the influence of Pierre Chareau, the French Modernist designer, to whom Arribas admits a debt.

RESTAURANTS AND SHOPS

A more obvious progression to his later neo-Baroque style can be seen in his design of the Electra fashion shop in 1987. A warm, highly polished teak floor, pedimented Classical pillars and moveable perforated metal screens vie with one another, creating an intentional conflict of styles. Elliptical shapes abound, in large mirrors in the changing rooms, curving wall lights, and patterns in the rough plasterwork.

Arribas' most publicized international commission is the result of his collaboration with Barcelona's favourite eccentric, the designer Javier Mariscal. A competition was organized by the government of Catalonia for the design of five little restaurant bars along Barcelona's new esplanade, Moll de la Fusta. For one of these, the tapas and seafood bar Gambrinus, Arribas and Mariscal have produced a relatively sober interior, with an elliptical counter decorated like a ship projecting into the middle of the room, which has furniture by Pepe Cortés. The mood is that of a first-class restaurant on an ocean liner, but the terrace, the site of a 'shipwreck', sets up a deliberate opposition. Here there are strangely shaped tables and chairs made out of 'driftwood' and light

The decorative interior of the lavatory pavilion at Louie Vega, a massive nightclub complex built beside a railway and overlooking the sea north of Barcelona, by Alfredo Arribas and Miguel Morte, 1988. Photo by Jordi Sarrá.

ABOVE *An Alice in Wonderland-style tunnel in crazy perspective, corridor of Elisava design school in Barcelona, by Alfredo Arribas, 1986. Stained wood cupboards are inclined backwards to give the impression of more space. Photo by Jordi Sarrá.*

LEFT *A cacophony of contrasting styles and clashing colours at Alfredo Arribas' Electra shop, 1987. A staircase up the rear wall leads nowhere, and the diagonally laid wooden floor plays with perspectives. Photo by Jordi Sarrá.*

INTERIOR DESIGN

The terrace restaurant of Gambrinus watched over by Javier Mariscal's cheeky lobster. Octopus and shellfish designs decorate the chairs; tables and parasols are roughly made of 'driftwood'.

The interior of Gambrinus, one of the restaurants along the new Moll de la Fusta promenade in Barcelona, by Javier Mariscal and Alfredo Arribas, 1988. The bar is shaped like a ship, and the mood is that of a twenties' ocean liner; furniture by Pepe Cortes. The overall scheme is by Manuel de Solá-Morales.

ABOVE RIGHT *La Cervecería del Moll by Grup CR. A slatted wooden bench runs the length of the bar, directors' chairs provide other seating. Slate floor tiles, wood and aluminium are the materials of this simple scheme.*

metal chairs with wrought-iron backs with a variety of Mariscal's cartoon-style sea-creatures – octopi, seagulls and fish. The umbrellas are roughly painted *à la* Robinson Crusoe. But the most remarkable feature of Gambrinus is Mariscal's giant 'friendly' lobster with its jolly lopsided smile and pincers outstretched in a welcoming hug, which is suspended invitingly over the restaurant and lit up at night. From the sublime to the irresistibly silly, nowhere else but in Barcelona would a project like this be funded by the government.

This complex of small restaurants, Los Chiringuitos del Moll de la Fusta, of which Gambrinus is one, is part of a larger scheme by the architect Manuel de Solá-Morales to re-unite Barcelona with the sea and maritime connections, particularly with a view to the 1992 Olympics. During the massive nineteenth-century expansion, the city built with its back to the sea, thus denying its roots, and there are now many projects aimed at reversing this trend. Los Chiringuitos might seem to be an unlikely venue: the dock with its yachts is some distance away across a wide promenade, and the esplanade itself is on top of a car park, with the Cinturon Litoral, the busiest part of the city's ring road, running below it. But it does work, and the four other restaurants, Traffic by Jordi Romeu, La Cervecería del Moll by Grup CR, Distrito Maritimo by Jaume

INTERIOR DESIGN

Castellvi and Blau Mari by Josep Croses, all completed in 1988, are busy and thriving.

The design of shops and their interiors is another great source of interest to the general public. High-fashion shops are frequented not only by top earners but also by ordinary people who will save or starve to buy designer-label clothing. With such a strong market for expensive clothes, retail interior design is especially important, and thus is worthy of serious investment.

Ideologically far from the fantasy and wilfulness of Barcelona, the Galician Adolfo Dominguez may have been the first fashion designer to discover this on a large scale. He has 300 shops in Spain and others in capital cities around the world, and he spends a great deal of time and money ensuring that they reflect his particular offer. His shops are designed by Santiago Seara and Alfredo Freixedo, and, like his clothing, are both austerely classic and severely modern, making use of materials like black marble, black iron grids for fittings and white walls, with huge mirrors very softly lit.

The Madrid architect Alberto Campo Baeza, working with Antonio Romero Fernández, refurbished the little Jesús del Pozo fashion shop with the aim of making it look larger. The façade onto the street has been completely glazed, and both the two long walls have been mirrored above a certain height. The featureless ceiling has been painted black, with rows of halogen lights which are reflected to infinity in the mirrors to give the impression of a vast starry sky. There are as few visual distractions as possible: only the simplest of fittings have been used, in black or white, and the floor is white marble. Thick sheet-metal doors, black-lacquered, form a forbidding obstacle to prospective thieves, but prospective clients are tempted by a thin slit across them, which provides a glimpse of the interior when the shop is closed.

For the interior of the shop A-2 (1987) in Manresa, Bages, Pepe Cortés chose a mixture of rough stone walls with smooth plaster bearing subtle frescoes. The ground floor has a marble floor, metal counter and basic metal shelving, and from it a staircase of sheet metal with a large curving handrail leads down to the basement. In excavating this room to provide greater height, some huge rock masses were uncovered, and these have been left in their natural state to add further texture to this very simple and understated interior.

One of the great strengths of Spanish interior designers is that they always seem to know when to stop. Original architectural features are respected, restored, spotlit, altered subtly to new uses and then left to their own devices. Fussiness is not admired, and neither is the language of the rural idyll which is seen so frequently in the 'grand country house' style of so many UK and US interiors – even domestic ones. Most Spanish commercial interiors are characterized by clean lines and sympathetic use of materials such as stone, marble and metals in a firmly cosmopolitan style, to be seen particularly in the public areas of banks, airports and office buildings.

INTERIOR DESIGN

S. CASILDA

FASHION

'Italy was famous for her rich materials: Spain for clothes of precise form and subtle line – in other words, the Spanish cut. . . . That distinction of line, that impeccable fit, so much the envy of fastidious persons all over Europe, was in its way a real expression of the Spanish gift for balancing discipline and vitality, fantasy and convention.'

(BRIAN READE, *THE DOMINANCE OF SPAIN 1550-1660*, HARRAP, 1951)

Santa Casilda El Olfato, one of a series on smell, taste and sight by Sigfrido Martín Begué, 1986. An ironic view of the 'saint of smell', herself being sniffed at by a dog, where the flowers are painted and fragrant and fetid smells are confused.

In the mid-sixteenth century, Spain was at the height of her power, stability and wealth. Just 50 years earlier, in 1492, Columbus had discovered the New World and offered it to his sovereigns Ferdinand and Isabella, whose marriage had joined the houses of Castille and Aragon and united Spain. The wealth that began to pour in from the gold and silver mines of the Americas funded a fantastically rich court and an accordingly lavish court life. The newly forged nation grew into a great empire under Ferdinand's grandson, Charles V, and Charles' son Philip II, who married the Catholic Queen Mary I of England, acceded to the Spanish throne in 1555, and then ruled for over 40 years an empire including Spain itself, the Netherlands and territories in northern Italy and the New World.

But Spain was a strict Catholic country – the Spanish Inquisition was at its most terrifying peak under Philip II – and although the court was certainly rich, clothing was modest rather than flirtatious. To compensate for this, it became more and more decorated and finely detailed, and the most exacting demands were put upon Spanish tailors, who acquired a high social status and a reputation for their skills around Europe. The influence of the Spanish style of dress and court life was very strong, for the first time rivalling that of Germany or Italy, and perhaps even overshadowing that of France.

The Spanish look was forged in those 100 years of wealth and inventiveness, and elements of it are clearly discernible today. The Spanish cut for women's clothing has natural shoulders and is body-skimming, like the Moorish high-buttoning coat. Fullness is traditionally

71

obtained by clever flaring rather than by gathering, which tends to produce a more bulky outline. The sixteenth-century Spanish farthingale – a hooped petticoat to fill out a conical skirt – infiltrated Europe, and for a time even influenced the English court, where gathered skirts had always been more popular. The flat and modestly covered chest, slim hips and very long waist of the period are also themes repeated in contemporary Spanish clothing. Northern Europeans, who tend to be more pearshaped, wear them at their peril. For men a slender boyish shape – that of a thinker rather than a doer – was and is still more popular than the inverted-triangle, 'he-man' silhouette.

The Spanish taste for black is traced by many scholars to the extended period of mourning that followed the death of Philip II at the end of the sixteenth century. Décolletage was also unpopular during these repressive Inquisition years, and there were strict rules governing women's street dress and the extent to which they should be covered. Many of these were inherited from the Arab world: in some parts of Spain, full-length cloaks or shawls had to be worn, which covered all clothing as well as the head, and had to be held across the face. All women except the lower classes were chaperoned, a tradition that lasted among the well-bred to within living memory.

Centuries of custom take their toll, and the necessity to cover up has resulted in two lasting fashion habits. One is the wearing of fringed shawls and lace mantillas, now reserved mainly for folk costume and elderly women in church, and the other is the classic Spanish knot of hair in the nape. This evolved partly from the need to secure the shawl with a comb, partly from the necessity of having a hairstyle which would not suffer from being covered, and partly from the pointlessness of contriving an over-elaborate hairstyle that no one would see.

The wearing of hats was traditionally reserved for the peasantry, and although hats have enjoyed periods of popularity through foreign influences, they are still far less common for formal dressing than elsewhere in Europe. The carrying of fans was probably inherited via the Romany gypsies from ancient Egypt, and coquetry and the language of fans eventually developed into an art which was taken up by the rest of Europe. Fans are still in common use, even among the young, but no longer carry the fashionable and symbolic significance of old.

COLOURS AND FABRICS

Apart from the traditional garment shapes and accessories, Spain also has its own colour palette to which many modern designers return constantly. These colours echo those of the country itself – sun-bleached mudbrick walls, oranges, olives, loam, sand, faded whitewash and the splash of red geraniums and roses. This earthy spectrum comes from the natural dyes first available to colour Spain's native cloths – principally silk and linen, followed by wool. For many years, blue dye was too expensive to use, even as a luxury. When chemical dyes were invented,

Regional costumes worn for the Festival of San Juan, in Javea. The rich brocade dresses, sequinned pinafores and elaborate lace mantillas are exclusive to the region, as are the coiled and combed hairstyles.

FASHION

blue was seen as a cold colour, and to this day has never been as popular in Spain as the warmer, more sensual hues. The bright colours of printed or aniline-dyed Indian cotton were never assimilated to the same extent as they were in England, since Spanish trade with India in the nineteenth century was minimal.

Silk originated in China and, before the secrets of its manufacture were discovered, was worth its weight in gold. In the eighth century, the Arab conquerors brought silkworms to be cultivated in the sympathetic climate of Andalucía, and by the time of the Christian reconquest in 1492 the silk business was firmly established across southern Spain, and was trading around the country. A century later, the ladies of Seville were famous for wearing only silk garments. The subtle colouring of silk reached a peak, with shades called, for example, *amigo triste* (sad friend) or *tiempo perdido* (lost time).

In the early 1600s, with Philip II's Armada destroyed, the empire was beginning to decline. A serious lack of international commerce had resulted from the small amount of trading carried out at the peak of the country's wealth. When Philip III expelled the Moriscos (converted

Moors) from Granada in 1609, he finished the work of his predecessor by virtually destroying the weaving industry which they ran. Imported fabrics and styles became popular again, and Spain lost its hold as a leader of fashion. But colour preferences and the strongly established Spanish look have persisted. These hundred years of wealth, power and self-confidence created a national style to express the spirit of the time, which somehow managed to survive nearly four hundred years of upheaval. The expertise in soft tailoring, the use of rich fabrics and the ability to produce delicate needlework are still in evidence today.

The cultivation of flax in Galicia also has a history going back to the earliest times. The town of Verin was the centre of an area which both grew flax and wove linen for the whole of Spain. This tradition continued right up to the 1960s, when Franco's isolationist policies forced local farmers to turn their land over to food production. The Spanish taste for the finest linens and linen tweed has persisted, and is currently satisfied by importing the cloth. One designer, Roberto Verinno, whose womens-wear business is based in Verin, is unhappy with this state of affairs. He is instigating a project to bring flax cultivation back to the region.

Traditional Andalucian costume emphasizes control – tight-fitting bodices for the women, tight trousers and boleros for the men – with dramatic display. These themes continue to run through contemporary Spanish fashion.

FASHION

THE FASHION INDUSTRY TODAY

As elsewhere in Europe, fashion was for centuries the concern only of the court, the nobility and the wealthy merchant families. Manual workers, farmers and peasants dressed in traditional clothing. In Spain this varied widely from region to region, and an experienced observer could place a traveller's home town by the style of headgear or the cut of a cape. Regional variations became less pronounced over the years, but traditional dress was the norm up to the last century, for all but the upper classes. It was not until the 1980s that high fashion became available to everyone.

A study was published in 1989 by the Ministry of Industry and Energy's *Centro de Promocion de Diseño y Moda* (Centre for the Promotion of Design and Fashion), on the changing buying habits of Spanish people over the previous four years. It was found that for modern Spanish consumers fashion epitomizes the new face of the country, and is bought for reasons of national pride – it is recognized as fully able to compete with that of other European countries. The selection of different styles and price ranges is enough to satisfy all tastes, and although many teenagers like US clothes, they can project a satisfactory US image with clothing made in Spain. Designer clothes are now everyday wear rather than being reserved for special occasions, and this fashion consciousness has spread from the cities into the smaller towns and villages. The popularity of designer clothes is a sign of a new social mobility, of people expressing their national culture and personal cultural awareness through what they wear. Demographic changes are giving a boost to the trend, with the bonus of a population bulge on the way for the late-teen to thirty-year-old age group – among the biggest spenders on fashion items.

The Spanish dote on their children, and are willing to spend a lot of money buying them good and fashionable clothes, so the childrenswear business is vital and growing, even though the birth rate is not. Fashion and party clothes for children are seen as essential, and new outfits for birthdays, saints' days, Christmas and Easter are almost obligatory. A huge annual childrenswear trade fair in Valencia includes a major section for design students, and a sponsored catwalk show. Most of the exhibitors export as well as selling to the national market, mainly to EEC and Arab countries, with the USA also a hungry market.

As formal recognition of the economic and cultural importance of Spanish fashion, the Ministry of Industry and Energy instituted the Cristóbal Balenciaga National Fashion Prizes in 1987. The Spaniard Balenciaga, who died in 1972, was described by Prudence Glynn in her book *Skin to Skin* (George Allen and Unwin, 1982) as 'probably the greatest tailor and architect of dress ever'. Many would agree. He began his career in Madrid, but after the Second World War he moved to Paris where he became a great couturier. He sculpted dresses around the body in ingenious, improbable but ultimately flattering shapes. He was responsible for many innovations, including the stand-away collar, three-quarter-length sleeves, the pillbox hat and the sack dress, and he trained the great Parisian couturiers Givenchy, Ungaro and Courrèges. In spite of his chosen home, he never abandoned his roots: McDowell's *Directory of Twentieth Century Fashion* (Muller, 1984) says of him that he was 'the true son of a strong country. He followed that long line of artists from Goya and Zurbarán to Miró and Picasso; his colours were those of the bullring, flamenco dancers and the Spanish earth; his cut reproduced the simple perfection of the monk's habit.'

The annual Balenciaga awards are granted in four categories: best Spanish creator; best international creator; best textile design company; and best new creator. They are very highly regarded, with prizes presented by the king or queen.

The Ministry is also behind a massive government campaign for the sponsorship of fashion. A major overhaul of the textile industry over a five-year period included providing interest-free loans for equipping factories with the latest machinery technology, giving subsidies for business expansion, and financing free management courses. The result of this scheme, which was wound down in 1988, was that, while imports

Classic fifties cocktail dress, Balenciaga style. Cristóbal Balenciaga is credited with being the inventor of this swinging shift dress shape; his models always wore gloves and the perfect accessories.

into Spain doubled over the period, exports of fabrics trebled. A similar scheme, which includes helping designers to exhibit at foreign fairs, is under way for fashion. One disadvantage of the project is that it has been set up to help companies which are already well-established and which have the necessary manufacturing back-up. Despite having the government's blessing, many designers still find it difficult to persuade staid Spanish bankers to support them, although things are slowly improving. So while the Ministry's tough criteria for entry to their scheme ensures that new buyers will always have their orders honoured, it excludes some highly creative designers who may need this exposure to encourage the financial investment necessary to establish themselves.

THE DESIGNERS

Arguably the most inventive of Spain's fashion designers is Sybilla, who won the first Balenciaga award in 1988, alongside Giorgio Armani. Still only in her 20s, many fashion writers acknowledge her as the world's leading creative designer. She was born in New York to a wealthy Anglo-Argentinian father and a Polish mother, Countess Sybilla, who had a couture business in Manhattan. The family moved to Madrid when Sybilla was a child. Straight after school, she went to Paris and worked at Yves Saint-Laurent for a year, where she learnt about craftsmanship. Returning to Madrid, she began designing shoes, her first love, then presented her first clothing collection at the age of 20 in 1983, at the height of media attention on La Movida in Madrid.

Her shapes and colours are always instantly recognizable, and she has virtually invented new sewing techniques. Like many Spanish designers, she loves earthy colours, and hers are always muted though powerful. She used to mix her own fabric dyes, but now has colours and fabrics made up exclusively for her. Her trademark is asymmetric ruching, gathering and bunching which, through inspired cutting, achieves a look of studied nonchalance. She pioneered the use of wired hems and soft metal stiffening in collars and reveres, which can be twisted into fantastic shapes – curves, concertinas, cabbage roses – elaborate but never less than elegant. She has also made clothes from basketweave, feathered stitching, fish-scale designs or plaits of fabric, and often uses padding to create relief patterns. Her soft tailoring is also superb, with seemingly impossible collar shapes and immaculate button closings.

In 1988 Sybilla signed up with Gibo, the Italian company which produces Jean-Paul Gaultier's clothing. She needed more serious financial backing to broaden her field of practice, and manufacturing capacity which could handle her exacting and specialized requirements on the production line – unfortunately not yet available in Spain. She has another deal with an Italian company which makes her shoes and handbags; she designs extraordinary hats, and produces a line of very beautiful bed linen, with appliqué and embroidery, for Bures, a company in Barcelona.

OPPOSITE PAGE *The model stands complacently in a Dali-inspired landscape, wearing Sybilla's white wired coat and olive dress of 1987. Photo by arguably Spain's foremost fashion photographer, Javier Vallhonrat.*

More Sybilla of 1987 with this jacket and skirt, at the peak of her wiring and padding phase. The high standards needed to execute these techniques finally drove her to production in Italy. Photo by Javier Vallhonrat.

FASHION

For many Spaniards, Sybilla symbolizes the future of Spanish fashion design. Although some chauvinistically refuse to accept her as a fellow-Spaniard, many would starve for a Sybilla dress, and have even coined a word based on her name. To describe something fresh and new, they say it is *sybillino*.

The second Balenciaga award winner, Jesús del Pozo, although also designing in a romantic vein, has a more technical background. Ten years older than Sybilla, he produced his first fashion work at a time when Spain was not yet ready for him. He was born in what is now Madrid's most fashionable street, where his father was a basket weaver. Inheriting manual dexterity, he began an industrial engineering course, but abandoned this for furniture and interior design, while also winning prizes for painting. After his military service at the beginning of the '70s, he satisfied his passion for clothing by having his tailor make him suits out of antique fabrics. His staid father was horrified, and burnt them, upon which del Pozo decided to leave Spain and travel. After two years, he returned to set up a menswear shop, eventually producing women's tailored clothes as well. After many years of struggle and near starvation,

Outlandish flowered evening cape and matching dress by Jesús del Pozo for his summer 1988 collection. This abundant cornucopia of flowers has been designed by the son of a basket-weaver.

BELOW *Austere Spanish lines, fitting the body to a low waist with fully flaring skirt, by Jesús del Pozo. Orchid-shaped cuff ties relieve the severity. Photo by Paco Rubio.*

ABOVE *Jesús del Pozo's fine silk dress tumbles around the statuesque model like waves breaking over rocks – a triumph of pattern-cutting. Photo by Paco Rubio.*

FASHION

he is now one of Spain's top designers, producing mainly womenswear, plus bed linen, towels and shoes. His style is classic, though characterized by intricate detailing.

Antonio Alvarado, sometimes called the Spanish Jean-Paul Gaultier, has a reputation for pushing out the boundaries of design while remaining meticulous about fabrics, cut, making up, finish and presentation. Originally from Alicante, he settled in Madrid in the early '70s, and was already up and running during the La Movida years. More definably modern than either Sybilla or del Pozo, he presents strongly themed collections, such as 'Tacon Amargo' (Bitter Heel) or 'Pecado Mortal' (Mortal Sin), and has a fascination for tattoos. Some of his inspiration comes from comics and '50s super-heroes: mildly perverse and sadistic themes are common. His clothes are aimed at tough but sexy and outgoing women, and clean-cut modern men. He designs all his own

OPPOSITE Antonio Alvarado's cheeky
schoolboy-cum-vamp look of 1988, in
his Tacon Amargo (bitter heel)
collection, with stiletto on tie. The feel
is aggressive and knowing.

ABOVE Spain's answer to the avant-
garde French designer Jean-Paul
Gaultier, Antonio Alvarado, shows his
menswear collection of 1987. The
skintight yellow buttoned leggings,
cropped jackets and cuban heels give a
swashbuckling pirate look.

Billowing folds of silk accentuate the model's slender shape in this subtly toned evening outfit by Victorio and Lucchino of 1989. A startling departure from the designers' former eccentric creations, this sensuous collection puzzled the press and confused their followers. Too beautiful to be fashion?

accessories, and made the clothes for Pedro Almodóvar's famous film *Matador*. Disappointed with the lack of potential investment in Spain he, like Sybilla, moved his production to Italy.

Victorio and Luchino, from Seville, are the only top designers to come out of the largest autonomous region, Andalucía, highlighting the cultural distinctions existing in this varied country. These two designers, whose real names are José Luís Medina and José Victor Rodriguez, live in the history-steeped ancient quarter of Seville, in the house where Diego Velázquez was born, which is furnished with furniture and artefacts of the period. For many years they created glamorous evening wear with a strong flamenco accent, but thoroughly modern elements, such as dinosaur spikes or wired skirts. One outfit recalled a watermelon, with a melon hat and a dress of green stripes with a pink dotted underskirt. Never silly or too extreme, these dresses were always immensely feminine and appealing.

In 1988 to 1989, Victorio and Luchino decided on a totally new direction. Concentrating on day wear, they came up with a collection of soft, draped clothes in very calm and subtle colours with a remarkable amount of clever detailing. Tiny buckles and clips, draped dresses with dolman sleeves or capes all made from a single piece of fabric, fantastic embroidery, unusual button flaps and edging details and a particularly fine selection of dresses and blouses in heavy Chinese silk made up this

Victorio and Lucchino as they first became known to the world, with a riot of frills, spots, frogging and contrast embroidery, in their evening wear collection of 1987.

The elongated fringes dangle with the full pleats of this silk evening dress, by Victorio and Lucchino, 1989. Deliberate play and accentuation of Spanish emblems is a regular feature of Spanish fashion design.

85

FASHION

Very low-key and relaxed menswear by Galicia's highly productive Adolfo Dominguez. Always influenced by Japanese designers, Dominguez uses rich sombre colours and loose unstructured cut, with dropped shoulders a regular theme. This fashionably rumpled suit with small-collared, high-buttoning shirt of 1989 is classic Dominguez.

collection. After years of frivolous fiesta frocks, Victorio and Luchino have arrived at a mature, sophisticated and strong line for the '90s.

The best-known of Spain's designers is certainly Adolfo Dominguez. Born and still resident in Galicia, the lushly green north-west corner of Spain, he is the first to acknowledge the meeting of northern and southern temperaments in his work. He studied literature and then philosophy in Paris, and has a rather cool academic view of clothing. He designs in spare but fluid lines, liking an almost total lack of ornamentation and little surface pattern; his clothing is often austere. He acknowledges the femininity of women but, in common with many Spanish men, hates blatant sexiness, which he believes is disrespectful of women. His menswear is distinctive and directional, but respectable enough for the Prime Minister to wear, as he often does.

Dominguez sees himself as an industrial designer filling a need, and believes that many designers wrongly try to impose their wills on their customers, and that this causes them to lose their way. He has a strict Bauhaus view of design, including clothing design, and would like to extend his philosophy of work into furniture and other home accessories, objects which people use every day. His fashion business is extremely successful. He has 300 outlets in Spain, another 100 in other parts of the globe, and his own shops in Paris, London and Hong Kong. He has become something of a recluse, living quietly with his family in his own architect-designed complex in a valley in Galicia.

Dominguez is another admirer of slender, statuesque women, as this dress with its Grecian statue folds suggests. Dominguez' womenswear is generally modest and understated but very feminine, unlike the Japanese who introduced the aggressive samurai shoulderpads of the middle 1980s. Strong but silent is the key, for the Dominguez woman and for his clothing.

FASHION

Dominguez is not the only designer to live in inspiring surroundings: Roser Marce of Barcelona both lives and works in Gaudí masterpieces. Like the Italians, the Spanish attach great importance to their working environments, believing that a good ambience will enhance their work. Roser Marce is an established designer with a large and vastly successful business, selling her women's and men's wear around the world.

She was another designer who entered the world of fashion from an oblique angle, having graduated in fine art. While at college she designed some knitwear just to support her artistic career, but was so successful that she switched to fashion, took a design course, and started up her own company. She uses only the best fabrics, many of them exclusive to her. Her look – well-cut suits with distinctive detailing – is for sophisticated careerists, and blouses with an endless succession of different and unusually shaped collars are her trademark. Her evening wear always modestly covers the body, perhaps an echo of her own shyness. Her softened masculine style is understated and always has an air of innocence.

Roser Marce' menswear, intended for men who can wear something a little different, but not too different, is immensely popular. There is a complete collection of cotton underwear for men, including the first-ever 'bodies' (all-in-one underwear) for men, which, apparently, are worn by fashion lovers and cabinet ministers alike. Her knitwear is still a major part of her business. She is an Anglophile, married to an Englishman, Peter Rogan, who is also her business partner.

NEAR RIGHT *Roser Marce's menswear in defiant flamenco pose, from her 1988 collection. The high-collared lurid green shirt and canary-painted tie with cropped fitted jacket and sailor's trousers is for the man who likes to make an ironic statement. The splashy painted backdrop is very Barcelona. Photo by José Manuel Ferrater.*

FAR RIGHT *Black evening dress with red hat, a typically surprising mixture of ordinary and extraordinary from Roser Marce. The slightly self-conscious childlike pout, along with the not-so-flattering highwaisted line, is for the well-heeled businesswoman who remembers childhood well enough not to take herself too seriously. Photo by José Manuel Ferrater.*

FASHION

Jordi Cuesta is another popular Barcelona designer who produces eminently wearable day clothes for professional women. Educated in Holland, he returned to Barcelona with a taste for the freedom of democratic Europe. He studied industrial design for a time, but was sidetracked into working in a top Barcelona boutique for five years. After his military service he moved to Venezuela and opened his own shop selling European designers' clothes. At the age of 23, with a wealth of experience already behind him, he returned to Barcelona to set up his own fashion company and he now sells all over Europe and in New York.

Cuesta is one of the most copied of Spanish designers, especially by the domestic mass market, but his own designs owe little to anyone else – he pulls fresh ideas out of his own head every time. He designs loosely structured clothes which can be fastened in a number of ways, and outfits in the softest Spanish leather. His main concern is to make women feel comfortable and feminine but secure (he does not want to undertake menswear). He is very cautious, determined to build up his reputation slowly and only sell to the number of wholesale customers he can service properly.

How many fashion designers have come through the disciplines of industrial design or even architecture? This last was the route employed by mens- and womenswear designer Antonio Miró, one of the older generation of fashion designers who have been in business since the '60s. He was the first Spanish designer to gain an international reputation and following. Applying architectural feeling to clothes, he constructs finely detailed but deceptively simple shapes, with a detectable Japanese influence. He has won many awards including the 1987 Balenciaga award for best Spanish originator, and has designed uniforms for the Olympic committee, the Barcelona metropolitan police and Barcelona's taxi drivers.

A touch of forties' Hollywood style in this outfit by Jordi Cuesta, 1989. Cuesta's women are assertive but superelegant, in the New York/Ralph Lauren mode.

Long lean lines by Jordi Cuesta, who achieves layering without any feeling of bulkiness with this long cardigan coat, and knee-length jumper over long skirt with shawl, of 1989.

FASHION

Miró believes that clothes should transcend time and occasion, and his lines, although modern, are austere rather than striking. Discretion and understatement are his trademarks, but his clothes are very beautifully made, with the high proportion of hand finishing, so common in contemporary Spanish fashion clothes. He is aware that men now buy their own clothes and take greater pleasure in them than in the past, and believes that men should be dressed simply but not traditionally. Unusual lapel shapes are a regular feature of his more tailored clothes.

One of the most financially successful of Spain's fashion companies is that of designer/manufacturer Roberto Verinno. Coming from a long line of tailors, he took over the family firm after studying art in Paris in the '60s. Having seen how the great couture houses of Paris were turning to ready-to-wear in order to increase their turnover, and having gained some experience working in a Paris boutique, he decided to reorientate the family business towards these new principles.

When he began this process, in 1970, he had great trouble persuading local women to come and work for him. His home town of Verín (from which he takes his name) in Galicia was a bastion of old Spain, and he had to talk to local priests and schoolteachers to persuade the girls and young women that it was respectable to work in his factory. He now employs some 300 local people, many of whom have been trained to operate the computerized processes of the industry.

LEFT *The immaculately executed fishscale fronted blouse by Antonio Miró of 1988. Despite the spectacular handiwork, the mood is low-key and thoughtful. Photo by Antoní Bernad.*

TOP RIGHT *Beautifully cut men's cardigan jacket by Antonio Miró, relaxed and slightly countrified. Photo by Antoní Bernad.*

BOTTOM RIGHT *An Edwardian feel with high long-pointed collar, high-buttoning waistcoat, narrow trousers and pumps. The collarless jacket is classic Miró. Photo by Antoní Bernad.*

FAR RIGHT *A stunning image by Antoní Bernad of Antonio Miró's wrapover blouse of 1989. The casually wrapped contrasting collar is reminiscent of Greek classical statuary.*

FASHION

Verinno's top-quality clothes are cut on tailoring principles, using the best fabrics, and with noble, slightly masculine and geometric lines. In 1983 he opened his first shop in Paris, the first Spanish designer to do so. He has collaborated with famous Spanish artists to produce limited-edition printed fabric patterns for special women's wear. He exports all over the world – he is opening a shop in Tokyo in late 1990 – and his turnover is well over a billion pesetas. He is responsible for many philanthropic ventures, including setting up local scholarships for economics, design and computer studies relating to fashion. He is founding a design school, and is trying to re-establish the local flax growing tradition.

Best known for his knitwear and clothing, Manuel Piña from La Mancha also designs shoes, handbags, jewellery and printed textiles. After a long apprenticeship working in fashion shops, and finally managing a knitwear workshop, he decided to create his own collections, starting in 1974. Now very much a Madrileño, he designs for a particular type of determined Madrid career woman, sometimes known by his name, as *la mujer Piña* (Piña woman). He uses a lot of black, for its drama and classicism, and because it gives women confidence and strength. He neither follows nor sets trends, but designs sober garments which he expects to be wearable for many years. Some of his evening wear, however, is almost sinfully sensual, though it could not be called simply sexy – *la mujer Piña* is always in control of her situation. A perfectionist, punishingly hard worker, a loner and ascetic, he almost killed himself with overwork at one time. Although not a church-goer, like many Spaniards he cannot deny the influence of religion, and once said, 'For

Belted raincoat with a Parisian air by Roberto Verinno, 1988. Due to the more temperate weather and to clothing habits, raincoats are not a staple item all over Spain as they are in wetter countries. Photo by Paco Rubio.

94

*Beautifully cut fully flared skirt in
wraparound hooded jacket by Roberto
Verinno, 1987. The flared skirt rather
than pleated or straight-cut skirts is a
major fashion emblem of Spain. Photo
by Paco Rubio.*

*Chic taupe sleeveless trousersuit in silk
by Roberto Verinno for summer 1989.
Photo by Paco Rubio.*

me religion and romanticism are water which wet the earth. Without water there can be no fruit, just dry land.'

In the Piña mould, but only in their mid-twenties, Luís Devota and Modesto Lomba design softly structured clothes in sombre colours. Modest but with unusual layering, they are reminiscent of medieval garments. Devota and Lomba believe in having a few key clothes: simple, modern but not trendy, and sufficiently well made to wear for a long time; their aesthetic is beauty rather than prettiness or frivolity. Devota, believing that the '90s will see a return to form, with austere lines and little decoration, says, 'We have lost the capacity to be shocked by the ultra-modern or by extravagance; that is in its death-throes.' It will be interesting to see if this prediction – very much in line with the reaction against Eighties materialism and indulgence – holds true for Spanish fashion in general during the Nineties.

JEWELLERY

This is the country's fastest growing export – almost too fast – with a 52 per cent increase in 1985 and a staggering 73 per cent the following year. The jewellery industry, including costume jewellery, is co-ordinated from the island of Menorca, where three-quarters of production originates. Spanish fashion jewellers are the most tight-knit group of manufacturers in Europe. They have employed, with additional government backing, a professional team to coordinate plans on commerce, marketing, technology, design, training and research in an aggressive four-year programme which began in 1988. The top fashion jewellers, while their output is limited, are a vital and inspiring part of this industry. Their radical, even shocking designs have given contemporary Spanish jewellery a high profile in the international market.

LEFT *Manual Piña's knock-'em-dead wedding dress of 1988. This wired lace dress (not for demure brides, as it is skin tight) is a play on the bata de cola, or exaggerated train of theatrical flamenco dresses. Photo by Javier Vallhonrat.*

ABOVE *The deliberately shapeless and sombre futuristic clothing of Luís Devota and Modesto Lomba, in this men's high-buttoning jacket and shirt for 1989.*

Elephant grey coat dress with medieval influence by Luís Devota and Modesto Lomba, 1989.

97

One of the leading protagonists is Chus Bures, who originally studied interior design in Barcelona. He worked for a while in London during the late '70s, when the club and punk scene were at their height, and these had a strong influence on his work. Moving to New York, he became involved in the Art Wear movement (wearable art), and continued producing some highly experimental pieces in non-precious and found materials. He then settled in Madrid, designing jewellery and accessories for Dora Herbst in crystal, aluminium, plastic and cork. From 1983, he collaborated with Manuel Piña on accessories for three collections, and then went on to design in rubber and leather, continuing his work with Dora Herbst. In 1985 he designed jewellery for Pedro Almodóvar's film *Matador* and for Juan Minon's *Luna de Agosto*.

He continued doing collections for jewellery companies, also designing under his own name, and working with fashion designer Alfredo Caral as well as for Loewe. He has exhibited at art galleries, as well as producing collections with totally contrasting themes. Influences range from ancient Egypt and Greece to the literature of Edgar Allan Poe and Lewis Carroll. He works intuitively, designing extraordinary, spiky, dangerous-looking jewellery, silver pieces so light they barely exist, and strange tribal or festishistic pieces. Until recently he has used mostly

silver, with agates, chalcedony and turquoise, to make unconventional pieces such as finger stalls, spirals that curve into the ear, and sunbursts that fit around the neck with matching earrings sticking out at right angles from the head. In 1989 he produced his first collection in gold and diamonds, and also opened his first shop in Madrid.

A designer of more solid pieces is Madrileño Joaquín Berao, who comes from a family of goldsmiths. His catalogues, which feature the work of photographer Javier Vallhonrat, are as much an art form as the work itself, which he describes as having 'sensual equilibrium'. Using mainly silver as a base, he pioneered the use in Spain of unusual materials such as titanium and niobium, and has experimented with bronze and bronze finishes to achieve different patinas. Always taking the forms of the human body as his starting point, his jewellery is highly sculptural, complementing the curve of arm, cheek or ear. Some of his larger monumental pieces exist as pieces of sculpture in their own right. Berao exports to the EEC and to all major capital cities around the world, and has three shops in Spain – the design of his Barcelona shop won an award – and one in Milan.

Chelo Sastre studied jewellery design at Massana School in Barcelona. She began by designing exclusive collections for Antonio Miró in the '60s

Verdigris jewellery by Chus Bures in naturalistic shapes, reminiscent of ancient Roman jewellery. In the La Movida years, Bures produced punk jewellery, inspired by periods living in London and New York. He used rubber, plastic, cardboard, and interestingly shaped pieces of junk, and was part of the Art Wear (wearable art) movement in New York. Photo by Paco Rubio.

Silver pin designed by Chus Bures to be worn in the film Matador, *by Pedro Almodóvar 1986. Almodóvar's films have all been style leaders, as he uses Spain's foremost interior designers and furniture makers, fashion designers and jewellers for his sets and costumes. Photo by Paco Rubio.*

99

FASHION

and '70s, and continues with this collaboration to this day, though she now works under her own name. She sold her first pieces outside Spain to a top gallery in New York; Paloma Picasso wore Chelo Sastre earrings at her wedding.

Sastre's preferred materials are silver and gold, and she designs for men as well as women, using very Minimalist forms. She likes jewellery to be flexible and simple, producing timeless pieces which do not so much follow fashion as co-exist with it. She has produced the definitive cufflinks, and the definitive jeans stud, which clips over a Levi's stud. Silver button covers and tie clips are also favourite pieces. A major influence on her work is Gaudí, and one of her collections was based on his mosaic shapes. In 1989 she produced a collection called El Oro de

LEFT *Fossil shell shaped earrings by Joaquín Berao. These are rather modest compared to many of his larger pieces, some of which approach sculpture. Berao's trademark is his use of lines and curves to accentuate the natural curves of the body. Photo by Javier Vallhonrat.*

BELOW *Venus de Milo with arms, adorned by Joaquín Berao's wrapped linen-look bracelets in silver. Photo by Javier Vallhonrat.*

RIGHT *Stunning image by Javier Vallhonrat of Joaquín Berao's exquisite earrings, which elongate the lobes of the ears, and necklace which nestles in the folds of the neck.*

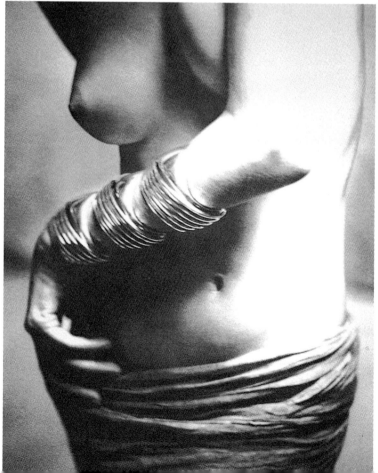

FASHION

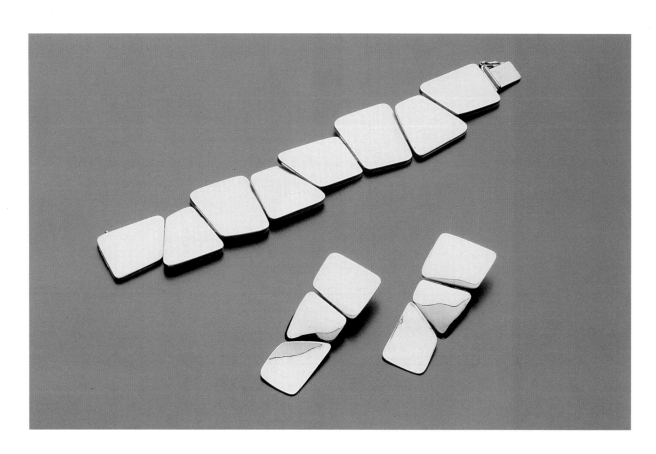

Earrings and bracelet in sterling silver
by Chelo Sastre. The sections are
uneven mosaic shapes, inspired by the
mosaics of Antoni Gaudí; hence the
name of this 1987 collection is
Gaudí. Like many of Spain's designers
who emerged in the early eighties,
Sastre is now considered respectable
and invited to produce collections for
old-established jewellery firms. Photo
by E Puigden-Golás.

Chelo Sastre for Soler Cabot, an established Barcelona jewellery firm. This was the first time the company had brought in an outside designer. She has also worked on pieces celebrating the Olympics, using the Olympic logos.

SHOES

The centre of the Spanish shoe industry is Valencia, with factories producing both mass-market and designer shoes. Sara Navarro is a highly original designer whose work shows Surrealist leanings. She acknowledges the influences of children's books and fairy stories, making fantasy shoes with twisted vamps, faces punched in the leather, platform heels and tassels fit for Aladdin. These unusually shaped shoes are decorated with kaleidoscope patterns or shapes derived from fireworks.

Navarro is also unusual in that she combines an extremely creative mind with remarkable academic and business achievements. She has a degree in Philosophy and Letters, having specialized in psychology, and

Chelo Sastre's essential Levi stud and button clips which pop over the existing buttons on jeans or shirt. Sastre is sufficiently highly regarded on the international scene to have been asked to create earrings for Paloma Picasso (herself a jewellery designer) for her wedding. Photo by E. Puigden-Golás.

103

FASHION

since becoming a shoe and accessory designer has continued studying, gaining a diploma for shoe styling at the Art Institute in Milan, and another for factory management from the Industrial Organization Society in Madrid. In 1980 she founded a prestigious annual literary prize in her name, and she returns periodically to study fine-art courses. Her three 'Sara Navarro' ranges account for some 50,000 pairs of shoes a year; she also designs a limited range of leather clothing. She is director of the group of companies to which Sara Navarro SA belongs, runs her own business and four shops, and has been commissioned to design all the leather accessories for the Expo 92 uniforms. This is no mean feat for a woman in her early 30s, and a classic example of the broad culture, exceptional capacity for hard work, and uncompromising nature of many of Spain's fashion designers.

NEAR RIGHT *Sara Navarro's slippers in mustard and burgundy suede, with cut designs borrowed from Halloween pumpkins. Navarro's rich colours are especially suited to suede. Photo by Galilea Nin.*

FAR RIGHT *Plush red suede shoes by Sara Navarro, inspired by the imagery of the story of Aladdin, complete with lamp. Photo by Galilea Nin.*

FASHION

106

GRAPHIC DESIGN

<In our consumer society, oranges must be painted orange in order to look like themselves. > (NORBERTO CHAVES, *ART BOOK II*, EDITORIAL PYGMALIÓN, 1985)

Around the middle of the nineteenth century, industrial expansion coupled with rapid technological advances revolutionized the printing industry in Spain. This was especially evident in Catalonia, where industry was booming and wealth and consumer spending were increasing hand in hand. The book-printing business, centred in Barcelona, profited particularly, and what had been a craft industry turned almost overnight to industrial production. Yet this industrialization was tempered by a vigorous appreciation of the ideas of William Morris as well as by the contemporary influence of international Art Nouveau, and finely bound and decorated books became immensely popular. This bibliophilic movement was part of the renaissance of the arts occurring around Europe, and by the 1890s Spanish printing and publishing – focused on the industrial centres of Catalonia, Valencia province, Andalucía and the Basque Country – could rival that of any European country.

Posters, first produced in the 1870s, became a hugely popular means through which fine artists could bring (and sell) their work to the masses. Only 20 years later posters had become sufficiently well-established as an art form to merit a major international exhibition in Barcelona, showing work by artists such as Aubrey Beardsley, Dudley Hardy and Spaniards Adría Guál and Ramón Casas. In 1898 two drinks companies, Anís del Mono and Champán Codorniú, were the first in Spain to use the medium to advertise their products. Posters and illustrated postcards continued to be popular, reflecting the vitality of the Modernist period, until the end of the first decade of the twentieth century.

Picasso's Bottle of Pernod, *now in the Hermitage collection, Leningrad. Painted in Paris, this shows the development from the early collage work of Georges Braque, who added newspaper cuttings and other graphics to his paintings.*

107

Art magazines also began to appear, influenced by the English review, *The Studio*, and by the various publications of the Parisian intelligentsia. Then in 1908 a new style of graphics, Noucentista (a Catalan word meaning 'new century-ism'), was born with the publication of the satirical magazine *Papitú*. The trademarks of Noucentista graphics were humour and the use of personalities to promote ideologies or advertise products. The characters were often lively and full of movement, in contrast to the languid poses of Art Nouveau.

The political climate of the time, under the repressive and anti-aristocratic military dictatorship of Primo de Rivera, had robbed the people of their enthusiasm for the heraldic devices that had been much used in earlier graphic work. Noucentista graphics, with its clean lines and simple forms in black and white, taking inspiration from Cubism, Futurism, and Dadaism, epitomized a new feeling, and became the vanguard of European graphics. The style continued to dominate until 1929 when the Barcelona International Exhibition brought in new elements taken from Art Deco.

ART AND POLITICS

The Civil War saw extensive use of posters, mainly by the Republican side. The Catalan government and the unions throughout the nation also used them, both for information and propaganda: at a time when other branches of the media were unreliable or subject to disruption, posters provided a spontaneous and direct channel of communication. There were around 200 poster artists working in Spain at this time, producing brightly coloured posters mainly in Futura type in a style that leant heavily on that of the Russian revolution. Cubism and Surrealism were put aside, and realism, satire and ridicule took their place. Such posters were exultantly patriotic, using direct and moving appeals to encourage recruitment to militias and the Popular Front, promoting aid to refugees and warning against spies and false rumours.

General Franco's reign was not a propitious period for graphic designers. Many who had been involved in anti-fascist campaigning or who did not want to live under his rule went to live abroad, while others found different professions, leaving few to teach or pass on their knowledge to younger generations. As Enric Satué said, in the design yearbook, *Art Book 1* (ed. Agustín Norberto Calabró, Editorial Pigmalión, 1985): 'The civil war deprived us of our natural grandparents.'

Throughout the Franco years, very little communication design existed or was called for, as enlightening the populace was never high on his political agenda. One of the few outlets for graphic designers was theatre and exhibition publicity, mainly posters. Josep Pla Narbona and Ricard Giralt Miracle were two major figures involved in these and other types of graphics at the time. Repression of certain types of publishing – in particular the thriving Catalan publishing houses – was widespread, and Catalan as a spoken language was actually prohibited for many years.

Poster for the administration of Granada commemorating the fiftieth anniversary of the death of the great poet, writer and musician Federico García Lorca. The images relate to the most characteristic symbols of Lorca – the moon, a horse, the Güardia Civil, and gypsy ballads. Designed by Enric Satué in 1986.

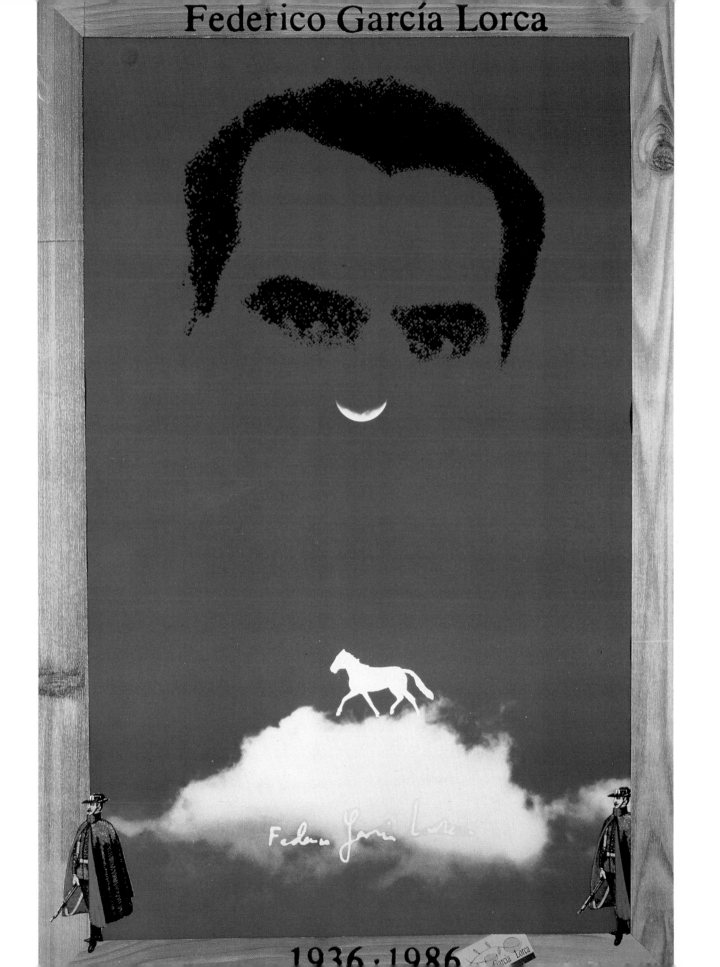

Federico García Lorca

1936·1986

109

Barcelona Posa't Guapa (*Barcelona make yourself beautiful*) poster for the administration's urban improvement campaign. The woman's face is made up from new features in the city – Norman Foster's telecommunications tower, Mariscal's lobster – and the balconies of a recently refurbished building. Designed by Enric Satué, 1989, computer designed by Animática.

GRAPHICS AFTER FRANCO

The advent of democracy in 1977 brought almost instant change. As Norberto Chaves put it in *Design In Catalonia* (BCD, 1988), there was 'an end to social silence'. The changed political situation demanded a fresh language to put itself across, and the newly created organizations and social services had to promote themselves by means of graphic output. The corporate identity, or public face, of these bodies is as important as their practical functions, and for this reason the State, the ministries and the autonomous institutions are the biggest employers of graphic designers in Spain. Information booklets, documents, forms, letterheads, logotypes and circulars are carefully planned to put their messages across clearly, reassure the public of their sincerity, and give an impression of the solidarity and permanence of the new organizations.

With the coming of the single European market, businesses are becoming increasingly international and handling greater competition. This has all happened very quickly, as international trading was severely restricted before 1975. As was the case 100 years ago, the vitality and optimism of the times is reflected in the wide range and high output of graphic material.

One of the best-known graphic designers in Spain is Enric Satué, who initially trained in fine art in '60s Barcelona. He has a typically Spanish outlook on his work, having always understood how to combine tradition with innovation, and he uses the latest technologies to make a design work on the most basic level. His annual report for the Banco de la Propiedad y Comercio of 1969 was a very early example of a process which became highly popular in the early '80s, that of die-cut. He used the same three-dimensional technique for *Cau* magazine from 1970 to 1974 – subsequently drastically watered down but nevertheless very influential. As Oriol Bohigas explains, 'creative inventiveness, the criticism of conventionalism, artistic revolution, result in models for the future, but at the same time collide with the difficulties of immediate acceptance'. Satué also cleverly manipulates traditional forms, re-interpreting with irony rather than pastiche. He has been the first to track and record the history of graphic design, and has written and lectured widely to broaden people's understanding of this richly cultural profession.

Among his well-known poster work is one he designed for the city of Granada in 1986 to mark the 50th anniversary of the assassination of Federico García Lorca. Using his illustration skills, he took the most characteristic symbols of the great poet and dramatist – the moon, a horse, the Güardia Civil and a gypsy singer – in a design which is both evocative and mournful. On a very different theme is a public poster for the Barcelona administration as part of a 1989 campaign to clean up the

Enric Satué's 1987 complete redesign of Spain's oldest newspaper Diari de Barcelona, *established in 1792. The first Spanish paper to use Century Expanded throughout, it was also planned to have a new masthead everyday, though this eventually proved to be too difficult to sustain. Photo by Enric Rion.*

111

GRAPHIC DESIGN

el Periódico
de Catalunya

city. Called 'Barcelona, posa't guapa' ('Barcelona make yourself beautiful'), it shows a woman's head made up of recent landmarks. She wears Norman Foster's telecommunications tower in her hair, her eyes are the balconied windows of a recently restored Modernist building, and her smile is Javier Mariscal's cheeky lobster from the restaurant, Gambrinus.

On a more sober note is Satué's famous redesign of *Diari de Barcelona*, the city's oldest newspaper, established in 1792. Unusually, the paper uses the same type face, Century Expanded, for both text and titles. It was originally intended to change its headline symbol every day, but this was continued for only the first year, 1987. Satué also updated the masthead for *El Periodico de Catalunya* magazine in 1989. In the same field is his corporate identity for the international press centre in Barcelona, the first of its kind in Spain, and funded by the Spanish government, the Catalan government and the administration of Barcelona. Set up in 1987, the centre has also attracted sponsorship from major manufacturing businesses in related high-technology industries.

Ricard Badía, who designs in similar fields, has also worked for the Catalan government's Department of Culture. For an exhibition and series of lectures called 'L'Epoca del Barroc' ('The Baroque Era') in 1983 his task was to project a strong identity with a design which retained its visual impact when used on posters and other material which had to carry a great deal of information. His classic poster for Design in Spain, an exhibition held in Brussels in 1985, was typically ironic in the Spanish fashion. Taking as his theme the famous fountain-statue known as the *mannéquin pis*, he expanded this symbol of Brussels in a very graphic manner. In 1986 the Department of Culture commissioned him to design an apolitical magazine called *Cultura* which, although now defunct, was a landmark of its time. As founder, publisher and art director of Columna publishers, Badía has designed many book covers since 1987, using illustrations, tints and black-and-white photographs, showing what he calls 'the post-Modern reality of our time'.

America Sanchez left Buenos Aires for Barcelona in 1965, and has since become virtually Catalan. He was co-founder in 1967 of the respected Eina Design School, where he continues to teach. His

TOP *Masthead for* El Periodico de Catalunya *by Enric Satué, 1989. The typestyle has been adapted from the existing established masthead for this popular Barcelona magazine.*

ABOVE *Corporate identity of 1987 by Enric Satué for Barcelona's international press centre, unique in that it is run by the city's College of Journalists and sponsored by central as well as local government. Photo by Miguel Gimeno.*

ABOVE *Identity for Barcelona's Department of Culture for the exhibition,* L'Època del Barroc, *by Ricard Badia, 1983. This identity won the Premio Laus of the year for its experimental use of typography, and the way dense use of the informative text has not detracted from its general impact.*

RIGHT *Bruxelles 85 Brussels poster for the Diseño-España exhibition in that city in 1985, part of Europalia. It is designed by Ricard Badia, and the reworking of the* mannequin pis *represents his view of Brussels from Barcelona.*

113

GRAPHIC DESIGN

specialities are corporate identities for companies and institutions and work on exhibitions and special events. He is also a recognized painter and photographer, working particularly with montage and manipulated images. His graphic work is extremely varied. In 1972 and 1973 he designed the now famous identity, still in use today, for the design shop Vinçon and its gallery, La Sala Vinçon. In 1984 he carried out similar work for the Barcelona Metropolitan Taxi Company, and he devised the famous symbol for the Barcelona '92 Olympic Committee. He has designed identities for male and female perfume, for the club KGB, and countless others for businesses and organizations. An interesting aspect of Sanchez's work is that it does not date: the Vinçon identity of 1972 is as fresh as that of KGB, executed 15 years later.

Tau is a Madrid graphic-design consultancy headed by Emilio Gil, who

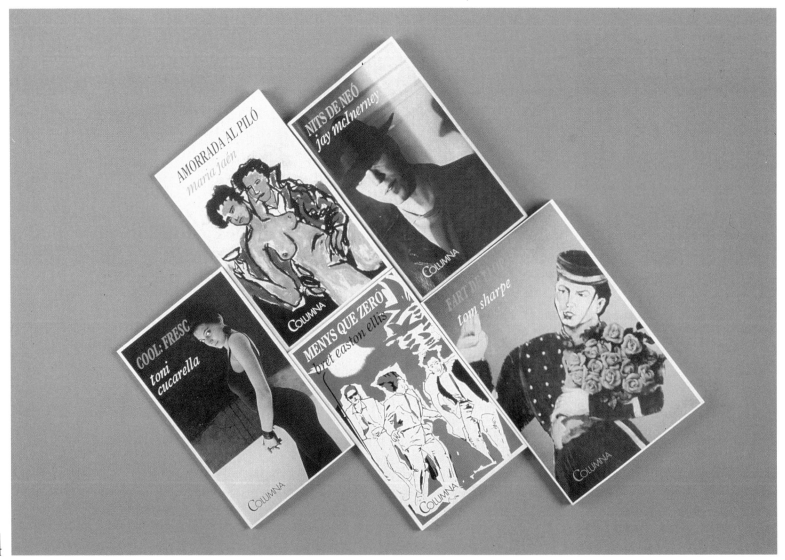

OPPOSITE, TOP *Ricard Badia's powerful design for* Revista Cultura *of 1986. This landmark magazine was funded and published by Catalonia's Department of Culture, but had complete editorial freedom and showed the most avant-garde and controversial work with impunity.* Cultura *ceased publication when funding ended.*

OPPOSITE, BOTTOM *Book covers for the modern fiction list from Badia's own publishing house, Columna Editorial. The tinted black and white photographs and illustrations show everyday images of the postmodern city and its people, reflecting contemporary reality.*

TOP *The timeless identity for Fernando Amat's shop Vinçon and its gallery, La Sala Vinçon designed by América Sánchez in 1972 and 1973 respectively. The logo is used to great effect on everything including carrier bags* RIGHT *illustrated by Javier Mariscal.*

RIGHT *Sánchez' identity for Barcelona's taxi company.*

VINÇON

GRAPHIC DESIGN

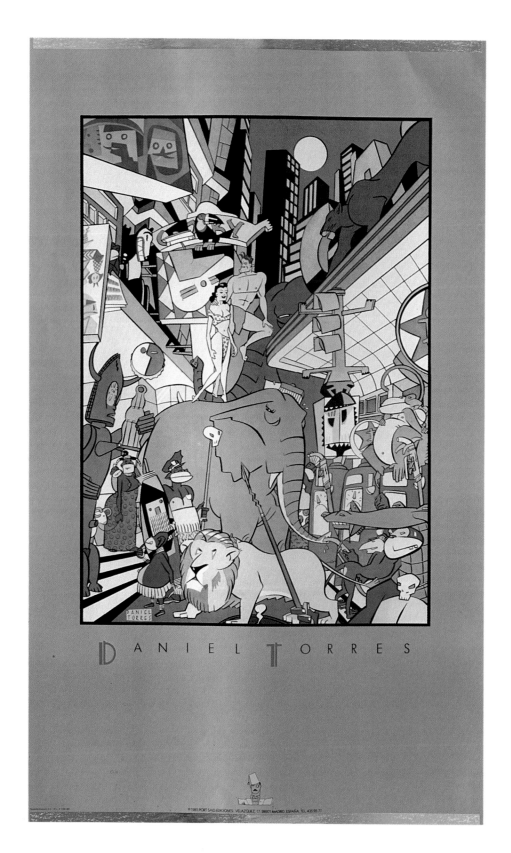

DANIEL TORRES

Poster for Port Said publishing house in Madrid. Port Said commissions the best avant-garde illustrators in Spain, such as Javier Mariscal, Ceesepe, Javier de Juan, and Daniel Torres who produced this view of the urban jungle. Port Said books are published around the world. Design by Emilio Gil of Tau Design.

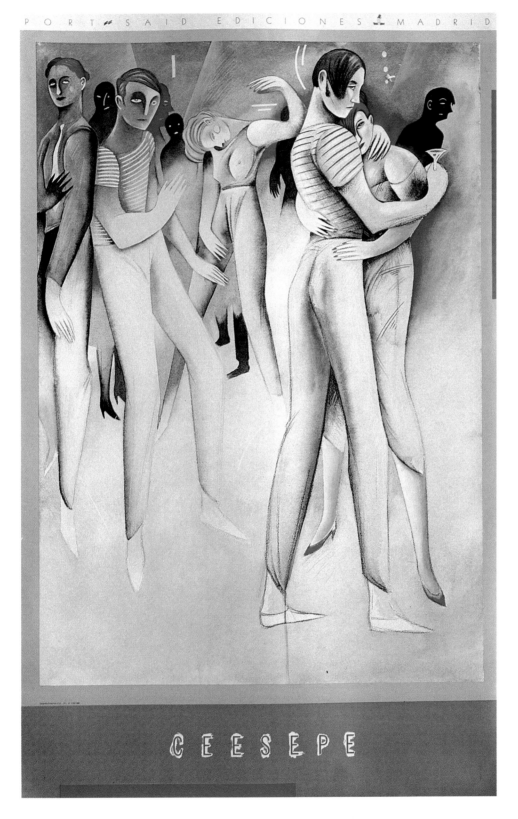

PORT SAID EDICIONES MADRID

CEESEPE

Poster for Port Said publishing house with illustrations of a night club scene, by Ceesepe. Comment on modern-day life, social problems and the stylocracy are recurrent themes in Spanish literature. Design by Emilio Gil of Tau Design.

GRAPHIC DESIGN

Design of total corporate identity for ICEX (Instituto de Commercio Exterior de España), which is responsible for promoting export of Spanish goods, including food and wines. These brochures and carrier bag are typical examples of the identity, which uses the colours of the Spanish flag in constant variations, and illustration evocative of the Spanish way of life.

was first trained as an architect and went on to study graphic design in New York. Because most of the other creative staff also studied architecture, Gil believes that Tau is better able to produce work of theoretical as well as aesthetic importance, which is permanent rather than transiently fashionable. Tau specializes in corporate identities, particularly for international companies involved in information technology. The consultancy is working also for ICEX, the export promotion institute, and for the ministries of Culture and of Industry and Energy.

One particularly impressive Tau design is that of *Sur Exprés*, a Madrid cultural magazine launched in 1987 by Borja Casani and his team. They had previously been responsible for *La Luna de Madrid*, the magazine of La Movida, the famous arts movement of the early '80s. *Sur Exprés* is very much *La Luna* grown up. Covering art, photography, fashion, design, literature and opinion, it conveys the spirit of the times in being intellectual and highly critical. Gil's design is simple and elegant but very strong, featuring drop capitals picked out in red, overlays and running headlines, giving it a very powerful identity which is also highly adaptable for showing many different kinds of avant-garde work.

Fernando Lopez Cobos is another graphic designer who has come through the disciplines of architecture and then of applied arts, which he studied in Seville. He moved to Madrid in 1974, where he began to work

OPPOSITE Covers and spread of Sur Exprés *magazine, which was launched in 1987 by the same team which published* La Luna de Madrid, *the magazine of La Movida. Both were designed by Emilio Gil of Tau Design.* Sur Exprés *is a showcase for leading artists, writers, photographers and thinkers, as well as designers and architects.*

118

GRAPHIC DESIGN

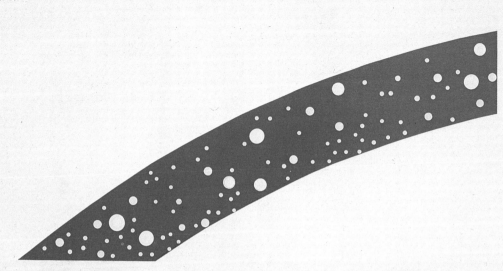

Museo de las Peregrinaciones

on editorial design and exhibitions, setting up his own studio in the early '80s to concentrate on exhibition posters and literature, and on exhibition design. The main features of López Cobos' work are the use of symbolic or evocative elements, together with an undemanding and apparently effortless application of typography. His identity of 1982 for the Museo de las Peregrinaciones ('Pilgrimage Museum') in Santiago de Compostela used the evocative symbol of the Milky Way. A poster celebrating an exhibition of 1985 on turn-of-the-century photography at the Museo Español de Arte Contemporáneo relied on the simplest typography to back up a particularly striking image.

His catalogue for the 1988 exhibition El Sueño Interrumpido de Miró ('Miró's Disturbed Dream') at the Casa de España in Paris uses as its cover image Miró's signature, the first letter of which is repeated as a drop capital thoughout the text. His elegant design of the guide to the Museo Nacional de Arte Romano at Mérida has been applied to all the state museums in Spain.

ACR, the graphic and design management consultancy of Xavier Corretje, Miquel Roig and Juan Carlos Arranz, specializes in corporate identity and packaging. Their look is very clean and simple, again backed up by very intelligent use of typography, and by marketing and management advice. ACR is one of only a few graphic-design consultancies which offer this service at present. Having no distinct style

Logo for the Museo de las Peregrinaciones (Pilgrimage Museum) at the famous shrine and place of pilgrimage at Santiago de Compostela, by Fernando López Cobos, 1982, for the Ministry of Culture. The illustration represents the Milky Way, and is used as a recurring theme around the museum.

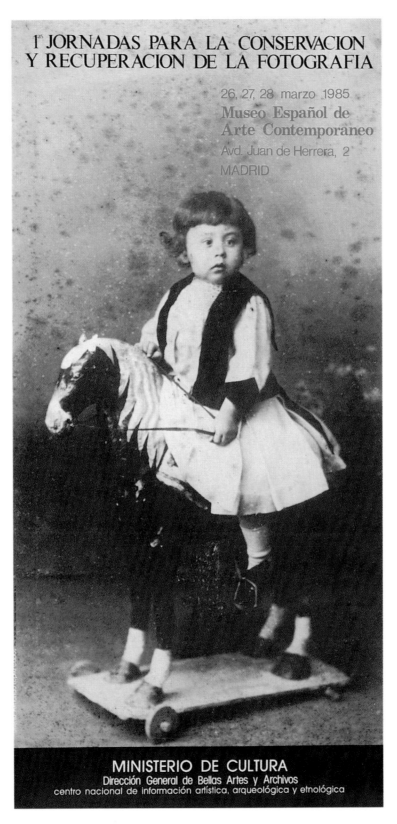

Poster publicizing an exhibition and conference on conserving and restoring photographs, by Fernando López Cobos for the Centro Nacional de Información Artistica, 1985. The simplest typeface and use of typography allows the arresting image to speak for itself.

GRAPHIC DESIGN

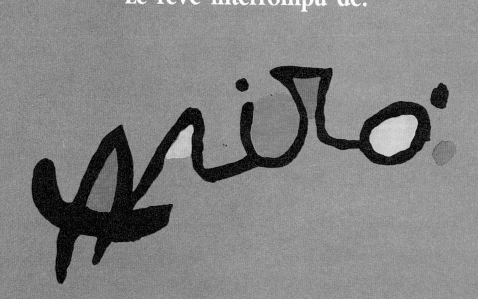

El sueño interrumpido de:

Le rêve interrompu de:

122

CASA DE ESPAÑA
Centre Culturel Espagnol

LEFT *Tastefully romantic packaging for Tu Y Yo, a popular brand of condoms which are now sold off the shelf – rather than from under it, if at all, as was the case in the past.*

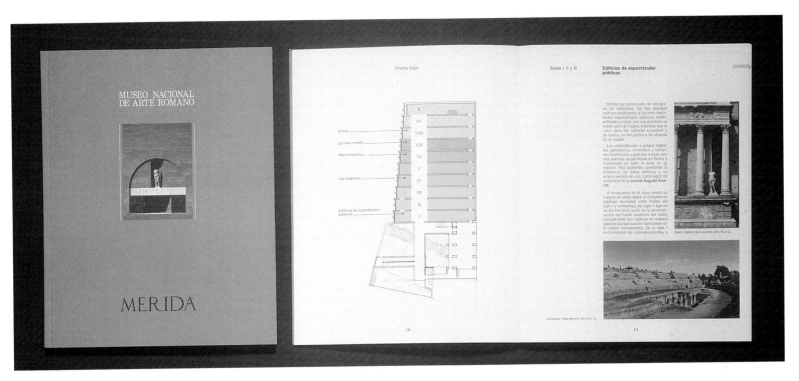

LEFT *Brochure for the paper manufacturer Sarrio designed around cutouts by Miquel Riog of ACR, one of many projects commissioned by the company.*

OPPOSITE PAGE *Cover for the catalogue of the exhibition* El Sueño Interrumpido de Miró *(Miró's interrupted dream), of the artist's work at the Casa de España in Paris, 1988. The use of Miró's own signature generates a powerful image. Design by Fernando López Cobos.*

ABOVE *López Cobos' 1988 design for the guide to the museum at Mérida (architect, Rafael Moneo). As with the catalogue* OPPOSITE, *an emblematic piece of work has been chosen for the cover image. The colour keyed plan of the museum is clearly shown in a design which has been applied to all Spanish state owned museums.*

123

GRAPHIC DESIGN

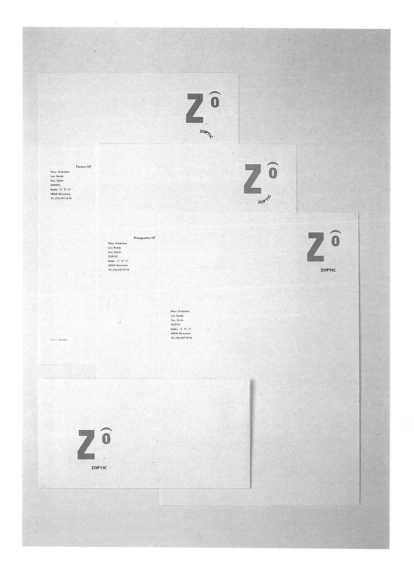

of their own, they operate very much on the lines of US and UK consultancies, and they have been responsible for creating identities for widely varied concerns – from hotel groups to condom manufacturers, from glue to hair mousse, and from ice cream to vinegar.

Mario Eskenazi, like América Sánchez, is an Argentinian who has settled in Barcelona, but who practised as an architect before moving on to graphics. He has had his own graphics studio since the mid-'70s, and produces a very wide range of work: pet-food packaging, book covers, an image for a bank, and another for a season at the Liceo Theatre, which was executed in collaboration with Sánchez. Stylistically, his work can be austerely simple but ironic, like his stationery for Zoptic, a video, computer design and animation company. It can also be witty, as seen in his designs for Nido, a pet-food company, which use a combination of cartoon characters and elegant typography. And it can be very cultured, an example being his image for the musical season 1988/89 sponsored by the pension-fund company, Fundació Caixa de Pensions.

According to the designer Alberto Corazón, the first corporate identity in history was created nearly 2000 years ago and has never needed to be updated. The symbolism of the Christian cross has permeated all four corners of the earth and is recognized by most of mankind. It is simple and easy to remember, can be adapted to all applications and needs no explanation – the symbol relates directly to the foundations of Christianity. A white cross on a red background, however, is instantly recognizable as Swiss. This symbol, still used today for innumerable Swiss products, was created in the days when the country's soldiers would hire themselves out as mercenaries for various wars, and needed instant identification at a distance.

It is this kind of immediate recognition that Corazón strives for in his work. The person in the street is constantly bombarded by so many different messages – audio, visual and graphic – that a simple process like trying to catch a bus can become a communicational nightmare. Corazón originally studied political science and economics before turning to graphic design in the '60s, which gives a clue to his approach to the subject. In 1987 he was asked to redesign the corporate identity as well as the complete signing and ticketing system for the Madrid transport system – underground, buses and trains – which he achieved successfully and according to his principles. Another identity is for the Instituto Nacional de Industria, a government body which represents a large number of manufacturers, for which he designed a three-dimensional symbol which suggests power, permanence and forward thinking.

Spain is at a very delicate moment, both politically and economically, and Corazón says that the face the country presents to the outside world must be that of competence and responsibility. One failed or frivolously designed project can create what he calls 'trails of mistrust' between the people and national institutions, or between the international market and Spanish business, which the country cannot afford to suffer.

The young design group, La Nave ('The Ship') could perhaps be compared to an '80s version of early Pentagram, the London group. Set

OPPOSITE, TOP *Stationery designed by Mario Eskenazi for Zoptic, a company working in the area of design in movement, such as video, computer-aided design and animation.*

OPPOSITE, BOTTOM *Brochure for Temporada Musical, a musical season funded by the Caixa de Pensions, designed by Mario Eskenazi.*

RIGHT *Mario Eskenazi's packaging for Nido Pet Food, complete with cartoon-style characters and text emphasizing the wholesomeness of the contents.*

RIGHT *Mario Eskenazi's packaging for Florsel tinned meats, with the surface design and use of typography suggesting something of a delicacy.*

GRAPHIC DESIGN

up in Valencia in 1984, there are 11 permanent members and a number of collaborators, working in architecture, industrial design, interiors and packaging, but they are probably best known for their imaginative graphic-design work. They work for a number of established organizations and government bodies without losing their sense of adventure and fun, and are called by *ARDI* magazine '. . . a breath of fresh air . . . the happiest and most promiscuous band of designers in the country'.

Their philosophy is largely one of avoiding boredom or repetition. 'We are seduced by intelligent ambiguity rather than by blind faith. We make no distinction between styling and technique, between aesthetics and function, between fashion and design, only between good and bad results. And we aren't worried about changing our minds and saying exactly the opposite if that's what we believe. We are alive.' This recent statement has the force of a manifesto.

Mingling avant-garde graphics and distorted typography with legible and simply defined copy is one of La Nave's trademarks. But their most recognizable feature is the use of pictograms. Their most ambitious work of this nature was for the famous Valencia Botanic Gardens in early 1988. Searching for a suitable symbol, they finally came across an organic shape by Matisse, reminiscent of an oak leaf. La Nave's Daniel Nebot had hit upon an unusual way of designing symbols, by sculpting them first in wood. The three-dimensional image, smoothed and polished, can then be converted into a two-dimensional symbol for graphic use. Nebot's Matisse shape has also been used for labelling plants and for the Gardens' signing system, while more direct use of his mini-sculptures is made in Valencia's technology park. Simple and elegant pictogrammatic shapes made up in relief in black stained wood have been applied to frosted glass circles which are backlit at night, and the same shapes, made up in metal, appear as directional signs, set into concrete strips in the pavement.

FAR LEFT *Cover for the magazine* **Retazos** *(cuttings) showing fabric colourways, for Seldis publishers. Designed by García de Paredes/ Amoros in 1979.*

LEFT *Cover for a report on olive production in Badajóz, part of a major survey. The illustration uses the image of a Spanish stamp to reinforce the importance of the crop to the country's economy. Design by García de Paredes/Amoros.*

One of many striking images using the Spanish national colours, this is the logo for the Spanish Women of the Year awards of 1986, organized by the magazine **Complice**. *Design by García de Paredes/Amoros.*

Las Españolas del Año
/86

127

Cover for El Víbora, *a pornographic magazine published in Barcelona, with this special cover feature on Javier Mariscal of 1987. His introduction to the design world was through strip cartoons, which he continues to produce between designing everything from shoes to interiors. The masthead is by América Sánchez. The exchange is: 'They're not biting', 'No, but they're having a good time'.*

On a more utilitarian note, La Nave designed the tourist signing for all the motorways in Valencia Province in 1986. Having decided that the system normally in use in Europe did not cover the vast wealth of sights that Valencia offers, they redesigned the entire system, using simple pictograms and illustrations more in keeping with the spirit of the region. It won them a top design prize that year, the Premio Laus.

Pati Nuñez also uses organic forms 'because I always wanted to be a biologist', but is strongly influenced by '40s imagery and typography and by Futurism. Barely in her thirties, she has been tremendously influential for some years, perhaps as much so as the UK's Neville Brody of *The Face*. A fellow graphic designer and occasional collaborator, Alfonso Sostres, said of her in 1985 that she adds 'speed and soul . . . in an order that is logical but emotive'. Her own aim is to make her work 'clean and easy, comprehensible to all kinds of eyes . . . sometimes the simplest solution, because it is unusual, can be the most novel.' Working for a wide variety of clients keeps her work fresh: she has many commissions for fashion and design projects, and likes to alternate them with others, such as corporate-identity work for an established institution. She claims she is very much inspired by nineteenth-century graphics (though you would never know it), and by Cocteau, Cassandre and Saul Bass. To keep her ideas uncontaminated, she avoids getting too immersed in the trappings of the world she often works in. She does not admire the manipulated graphics which can be produced by computer, preferring to return to original versions of typefaces and recreating them painstakingly by hand. She believes that photocomposition allows people into the profession who do not have a sufficiently knowledgeable background to produce good work.

A play on words gave Nuñez the inspiration for the identity of the yarn manufacturer Araño. An *araña* is a spider, which of course also makes thread, so a stylized spider was the natural choice for the symbol. Another play on words was used on one of many designs for the carrier bags of Vinçon, the designer shop. Using portraits of the proprietors by Javier Mariscal, Nuñez added the line *sociedad no anónima* ('un-anonymous society'), the term for a limited company being *sociedad anónima*.

She has completed two corporate identities in collaboration with Alfonso Sostres, one for a nightclub and the other for a café restaurant. That for the club, Otto Zutz, was conceived in 1985 with a stark, very Germanic tone, using striking black, white and red type. Cassandre's sailor of 1942 is the inspiration for the symbol of Network Café, in a clear and respectful allusion to the '40s.

That prodigious designer Javier Mariscal is also well-known in the world of graphic design, but more in the area of illustration than of typography and corporate identity. Mariscal has been an established cartoonist for many years with his *Julián, el perro pescador* ('Julian, the fishing dog'), who has many adventures on the seafront with his two friends, Fermín and Piker, and of course a great number of Mariscal's favourite creatures, lobsters. Julián has become famous enough to be manufactured in aluminium and sold in the design shop, Galerías Vinçon,

DE DISEÑO

REVISTA ILUSTRADA DE
DISEÑO INDUSTRIAL,
INTERIORISMO,
GRAFISMO,
ARTE Y MODA.
NÚMERO 10
MONOGRAFÍA
1.000 PESETAS (IVA incluido)

MARISCAL

The unkempt and irrepressible Javier
Mariscal, as he appeared in a 1987
edition of De Diseño magazine
which was devoted to his work. The
world-weary but penetrating gaze
belongs to undoubtedly the most
prolific designer in Spain, working in
virtually every field of design, as well
as in fine art. The signature and
cartoon mouse are by his hand.

129

GRAPHIC DESIGN

BELOW *An example of Mariscal's illustration work, much of which is sold as fine art and exhibited in top galleries around Spain. His rather childlike scrawl and distorted perspective are unmistakable.*

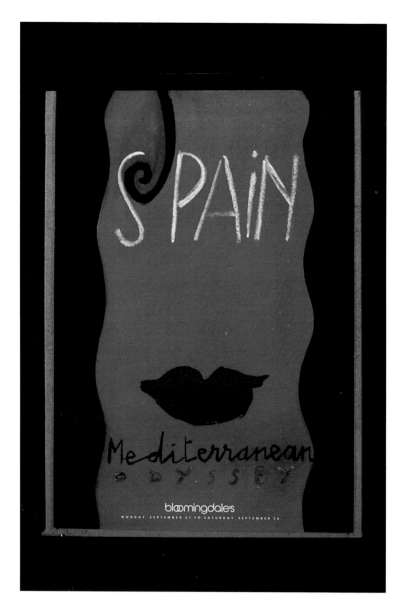

Poster by Mariscal for Bloomingdale's of New York to publicize their Spanish promotion of 1988. Mariscal returns to the clichéd images of Spanish women – the pout, the lock of hair – while the word Spain replaces sunglasses.

Poster design by Peret for La Biennal 1985, another play on Spanish imagery, that of the bull. Much of Peret's work recalls that of Cassandre, particularly his use of primary colours and strong geometric shapes.

as a design accessory. Another Mariscal creation, Cobi, has been awarded the ultimate accolade in a restricted competition organized by the Olympic committee – he has been named the 1992 Olympic mascot. Mariscal's rough, child-like illustrations have been used many times for posters and all kinds of promotional literature, with his unmistakable scrawling handwriting used instead of formal typography.

Peret (Pedro Torrent) also works in Barcelona, but began his career in Paris where he stayed for some years before settling in his native city. He combines typography with his illustration, which is of the simplest kind, in block colours, reminiscent of that of Cassandre. One of his most famous posters was that for an exhibition called 'Tintin in Barcelona' for the Fundación Joan Miró. For this he simplified the head of Tintin, the boy hero of the famous French books, into near-abstract shapes, but without losing any of the boy's charm. He has produced many posters for the Barcelona administration, and has worked on graphics for television and for *La Vanguardia* newspaper.

A restricted competition was held in 1988 to create a new identity for Eureka, an organization which helps European countries to cooperate on industrial, technological and scientific research to create new products for the international market. Peret's design used the Greek letter sigma, which symbolizes the sum of cooperation between participating countries. The sign for sigma is also very similar to a capital 'E' for Eureka. The exclamation mark, as well as giving emphasis, is used as visual reinforcement for the sigma. There is also a natural association with the legend of the exclamation made by Archimedes in his bath on discovering the law of displacement of bodies, Archimedes' Principle.

GRAPHIC DESIGN

FURNITURE

‚*It is heroic to live on the frontier, without prejudices or preconceived ideas. I could write endlessly about all those who have made design the dominion of restlessness.* ‚

(JESÚS MARTÍNEZ CLARÀ, *DISEÑO EN ESPAÑA* (MINISTRY OF INDUSTRY AND ENERGY, 1985))

Historically speaking, Spanish furniture design has never been considered as either particularly influential or highly original. It is true that there are very few great masters of furniture design who could be called to name. But there are specific pieces which can be traced back to Spain, and there was and still is a distinctive Spanish style which has permeated Europe at certain periods. Naturally enough, one of these periods was at the height of the country's wealth and power, in the sixteenth and seventeenth centuries, when Spanish or Spanish-style pieces were mentioned in inventories of great European houses, often referring to their intricate Moorish carving.

Medieval furniture was designed to accommodate the nomadic lifestyle of the people, caused by frequent wars between kingdoms and by the customary wintering and summering migrations. This persisted until the eighteenth century: everything had to be portable; clothing was kept in chests; tables were made to sit on trestles, and the few chairs that did exist were folding and likely to be used only by the heads of the family. It is thought that the scissor folding chair, a pattern which continues to inspire modern designers and was originally used only for kings and bishops, originated in Visigothic Spain. Over the next few centuries this chair evolved, with technical improvements, until by the time of Ferdinand and Isabella in the late 1400s it had turned into one with a wooden frame in the form of two back-to-back Cs, with a leather seat and no back. It is usually referred to as a Mudéjar hip chair. The wooden frame was often inlayed with marquetry by the skilled Moorish craftsmen.

OPPOSITE *Eduardo Chillido's* Gnomon III *sculpture of 1984. Chillido creates forms which are interpretations of three-dimensional Moorish key patterns, or Mayan-inspired carved stone. This chair-like piece, roughly a metre square, is made of steel.*

133

The *frailero*, or monk's chair, originated in Italy, but was absorbed into Spanish life during the sixteenth century. This has a square frame with arms and back, but with a leather seat and back so that it can be folded. Cordoban leather workers, famous for their intricately stamped and dyed leather wallcovering, produced particular designs such as cushioning, which made the chairs more comfortable but kept the leather flexible. The monk's chair, strongly associated with Spain, soon began to make its appearance around Europe, and it also went to the Americas with the missionaries, where it became known as a *missional*. The same pattern, now with a solid frame and solid leather seat and back, is still reproduced as a Spanish-style dining chair, and many examples can be seen in the Hispanic Americas as well as around Europe. An adaptation, folding but with canvas back and seat, has been used for over a century as a garden chair, and became the fashionable 'director's chair' of the '70s.

Possibly the single most important Spanish contribution to furniture design evolved from the humble travelling chest. Moorish craftsmen gave more and more elaborate treatment to the panels, inlaying with bone, metals and contrasting wood fragments. Every surface had to be decorated. Drawers, a Moorish invention, were introduced to hold smaller items in a wide lip just below the lid. This construction was common in the sixteenth century, but as it was rather awkward, a new version was devised, with all the drawers in one section of the chest, on one plane facing outwards. This had a folding lid to protect the drawers, while a second section was either like an ordinary chest or had front-opening doors. The exteriors were carved but robust, often enclosed with forged metal straps, but the interiors were very elaborately decorated. When the drawer section was placed on top of the chest, the folding lid formed a writing surface. This, the Spanish *bargueño*, became

OPPOSITE *The Gavina stool, inspired by the Visigothic scissor chair, though with the curve in an opposite direction. It was designed and manufactured by Jaime Tressera in 1988.*

RIGHT *A faithful reproduction of the Calvet armchair, designed by Antoni Gaudí in 1902. The chair is manufactured by BD Ediciones de Diseño, made entirely by hand using traditional materials and techniques.*

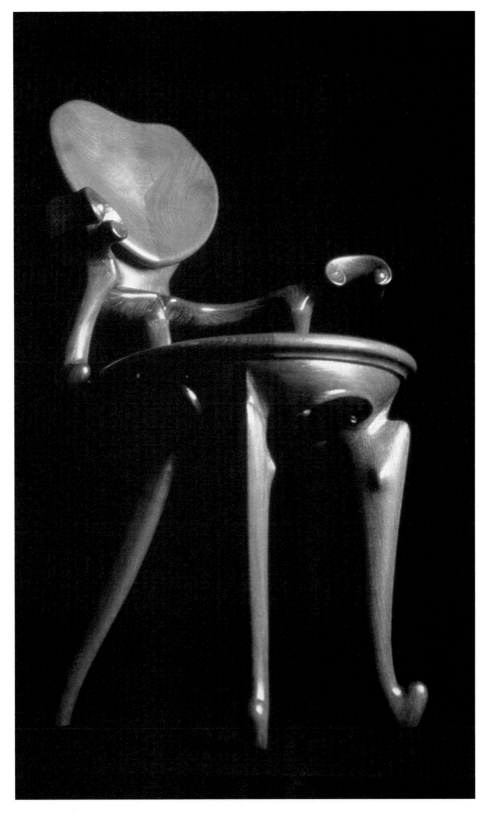

135

FURNITURE

Sixteenth-century **bargueño,** *the upper side handles showing clearly that it was made in two sections. The elaborate inlay, carving, painting and gold leaf decoration are typical of the period. The upper section would have had a solid, less decorated, lockable wooden flap, which is missing.*

the European escritoire or writing desk of the seventeenth century, antecedent of virtually every writing desk to this day.

The next period of great artistic activity came about in reaction to Spain's industrial revolution, centred on Barcelona. The last two decades of the nineteenth century saw great technical advances in furniture production, and this, as in other countries, gave rise to divergent artistic philosophies. There were many Spanish followers of William Morris and John Ruskin and (rather later than in Britain) there began a movement to return to craftsmanship, with the medieval period as its inspiration. Antoni Gaudí, while agreeing with their principles, had his own aesthetic, a rejection of the straight lines of mechanized production in favour of organic curves which could only be made by hand. But while Gaudí used so-called 'poor' materials such as brick instead of stone where appropriate, and broken tiles or china for decoration, designers in other parts of the country integrated traditional regional decorative elements. They were all seeking a new national art.

The architect Lluís Domènech í Montaner, the contemporary of Gaudí, and responsible for many buildings at this time, set up a workshop for artisans to rediscover medieval methods of ironwork, stained glass, sculpture, tiles and most especially furniture. Gaspar Homar and Joan Busquets were leading lights of this movement and used artists to execute or design the elaborate decoration required, such as japanning, painting and especially inlaying, very much influenced by Art Nouveau. Gaudí's own workshop devoted itself to similar projects, its crowning glory being the building, decoration and furnishing of the Casa Calvet, for which he designed his famous Calvet chair.

Rivalry between these designer-craftsmen and the exponents of Modernism was fierce, and the contrasting styles became further polarized over the following 20 years, coming to a head at the time of the 1929 International Exhibition in Barcelona. The administration favoured the style of Le Corbusier and Mies van der Rohe, epitomized by the famous German Pavilion, designed by Mies, and his Barcelona chair. The official designers' organization, Fomento de las Artes Decorativas (FAD), tended towards the Art Deco style, which was also more popular with the general public.

Spain's contribution to the European art and design scene was abruptly terminated in 1936 with the outbreak of civil war, and a long period of serious introspection followed, coupled with economic pressures which made advances very difficult. In the boom years of the '60s, and at the beginning of the '70s, furniture showed its machine origins very clearly, even mimicking the aesthetics of the machines and factories themselves – High Tech. But more recently designers have come to terms with the new technology in different ways, as it has become more sophisticated.

Modern machines can produce beautifully sculpted wooden furniture, complex upholstery, and finishes previously only possible by hand. Artistic and highly creative work is no longer solely the province of the hand craftsman, and many designers work for this kind of mass production as well as designing limited editions or one-off experimental pieces. These are often sponsored by manufacturers of new materials and made specifically to be shown in avant-garde exhibitions. And, as can be seen in these exhibitions as well as in trade fairs of mass-produced furniture, Spanish furniture design is characterized by a combination of an understanding of everyday needs with a constant critical re-assessment of preconceptions. While showing some stylistic similarities with that of Italy, it has its own recognizable look. Some Spanish designers worked for Memphis or were influenced by the Milanese movement, but for most it was a brief flirtation rather than a long-standing relationship. Geometric forms are common, but there is less dependence on the horizontal rectangular plane than in Italian and much northern-European furniture. Visual puns and Surrealist references abound but, although Spanish furniture is often fun, it is never foolish. In response to the small spaces available in many homes, much of it is light and compact, sometimes with a characteristically ingenious multi-use or foldaway features.

THE FURNITURE MARKET TODAY

The buying patterns of Spanish people have changed radically over the past 20 years. In the past, young couples would have bought most of their furniture, probably in a local rustic or traditional reproduction style, when they married, intending it to last all their lives. These days, more young people are leaving home to set up single households; if and when they do marry, a good-sized apartment in many regions and cities in Spain can be rented quite cheaply and with security of tenure. The tradition of home buying, with its attendant financial burdens, is less common than in Britain, which means there is more cash to spare for decorating and furnishing. The Spanish are enormously proud of their homes, indeed if given the chance they will conduct a visitor on a guided tour, relating the history and pedigree of every ornament, picture and piece of furniture. Keeping up appearances is immensely important, even to families with children, and they love to buy the latest modern furniture, both to enjoy it themselves and to show it off to their friends.

For these reasons the domestic furniture market is very strong, with some manufacturers during the mid-'80s reporting a doubling of their output every year. Now that this spurt of growth has slowed down to a more manageable pace, they have become well-coordinated and are working from a very solid organizational background to build on their first great successes.

When writing about furniture design, it is difficult to decide whether to start with the manufacturers or the designers. Really they are co-stars, but what is perhaps most important of all is the spirit which has nurtured the close collaborations between the two. Some designers would undoubtedly disagree, demanding even greater cooperation and understanding; they cannot realize how lucky they are. Spanish designers are in the fortunate position of being able to find all the expertise they need at home; they do not have to make long treks in order to find a sympathetic manufacturer capable of producing a particular design. Every manufacturer specializes in certain techniques and certain stylistic variations. Either he will commission a range of furniture from a certain designer, or a designer with an idea can select a suitably willing and able manufacturer. Many of the manufacturers' names are as well-known as the designers', and they have excellent marketing and distribution networks as well.

Another reason for the health and creativity of the market is that there is no strict delineation between contract and domestic furniture. This means both that highly creative pieces are often used in office environments, and that there is a more human language for specified office equipment, which can often be used equally well in the home. Many of the manufacturing companies are relatively small-scale, without access to the heavy investment they would need to equip themselves with the most advanced high technology, so they push out the boundaries as far as possible, making the best creative use of what processes they have. As is often seen in all branches of design, the tighter the restrictions, the better the end result. Bent and tubular steel furniture is common, with these materials often used in a revolutionary way, and traditional woodworking skills are frequently employed on designer furniture. Prices are reasonable and many experts believe that the Spanish market will be approached more and more frequently for orders for domestic-oriented furniture for contract use.

The organization SIDI (Salón Internacional de Diseño del Equipamiento para el Habitát), set up for the commercial and cultural promotion of design, both nationally and internationally, has this aim very much in mind. SIDI was founded in 1984 within the organization ON Centro de Diseño, which publishes *ON Diseño* magazine. It was recognized firstly that there was a growing band of manufacturers using top designers, and secondly that this section was under-exploited and

under-exposed. It is hoped that other mass-market manufacturers might be encouraged to buy in design, given the example of a well-run and financially successful organization. At the Milan Furniture Fair in 1988, SIDI celebrated its fifth anniversary and its 27th show, with a total of almost 60 members.

SIDI is an autonomous institution whose directors are María Carmen Ferrer and Carmen Llopis. Design content, quality of manufacture and customer service are the criteria by which members are chosen for inclusion. A prime force in setting SIDI in motion was the recognition of the existence of inspired management within manufacturing firms who were encouraging innovatory processes and buying the services of designers. Funded entirely by its members, and working through the medium of trade fairs, it has shown how to make best use of the opportunities these present: the SIDI stand is really an individual showroom within the context of a fair. The first one had a distinctive design by Alberto Liévore and Jorge Pensi. Both functional and noticeable at a distance, it saw the organization through 25 fairs. The later re-design is equally impressive. The provision of ample stocks of information packs for the press and the buyers as well as generous hand-outs of colour transparencies to magazines ensure that press coverage is extensive and that European buyers have all the specifications they need. For many such people, contact with SIDI at trade fairs is the only regular one they have with the Spanish people, and has successfully dispelled any former prejudices about the Spanish nation.

And it is other Europeans that SIDI is trying to impress at present, though some believe that the USA could present sufficient scope to be an attractive prospect for the future. The home market is by far the largest, representing around two-thirds of manufacturing output. After that come West Germany, France and Belgium, with Italy lagging behind, mainly because of their own large and varied market, but perhaps also because of the traditional rivalry between the two Latin countries. Like the Spanish, all these nations buy heavily for domestic use, whereas the British market is much stronger on the contract side.

Many Spanish manufacturers are overwhelmed and some even alarmed by the degree of interest shown by foreign press and buyers: it all happened so very quickly. They feel that the necessity of producing even more spectacular pieces every year could wear them out – there are those who think that this has happened to some Italian manufacturers. But perhaps the Spanish have learnt some useful lessons by watching the progress of Italy. The majority believe that in the long term it is more important to continue producing well-made pieces with a high design content, competitively priced, aesthetically pleasing and functionally sound. The furniture business becomes more like the fashion business each year, and they do not want to fall into the same traps, preferring to consolidate their quickly gained position rather than produce fantasy furniture for magazine covers.

Although Europe remains an important target for SIDI, Spain is the major market, and it also exhibits regularly in Barcelona, Madrid and

Continuity and craftsmanship have characterized Spain's furniture-making tradition: the seventeenth-century walnut chair from Mallorca LEFT *shows clear kinship with the cheerfully polychrome nineteenth-century example from Seville* RIGHT

Oscar Tusquets' audio and TV cabinet of 1988, manufactured by Artespaña. The Deco-style sunburst surface pattern has been made traditionally by hand using wood inlays. Decoration and historical reference are two of his favourite tools.

La Luna (moon) rug designed by Oscar Tusquets in 1987, showing the quarter moon. Accurate geographical details are woven into the design, which is remarkably sympathetic to its medium. Photo by Lluís Casals.

Valencia, all of which are centres of the furniture industry, and has also shown domestic furniture in small exhibitions for the general public. With a policy of constantly reviewing its aims in accordance with changing trends in the market, it is likely to grow and prosper for some years to come.

THE DESIGNERS

A regular exhibitor with SIDI is BD (Barcelona Diseño). In 1964 Estudio Per was formed by architects Oscar Tusquets Blanca, Pep Bonet, Cristián Cirici and Lluís Clotet, as an architectural practice for those who also wanted to produce furniture but could not find suitable manufacturers. A small workshop was set up to make the objects not then obtainable on the market. Nearly ten years later, Tusquets and Javier Carulla set up BD as a manufacturing company to work alongside Estudio Per.

Together with Estudio Per, BD began to work on experimental and adventurous designs in furniture as well as industrial and architectural projects. They have now broadened their field to include accessories, rugs, lighting and architectural hardware, and run a large studio of designers as well as commissioning particular designers for specific projects. Fine artists such as Guillermo Perez Villalta have designed exclusive rugs, and they have shown exhibitions of specially commissioned work on chosen themes.

Tusquets himself falls between the generation of design pioneers such as André Ricard and Miguel Milá, who founded FAD (Fomento de les Artes Decorativas), and today's more carefree generation. A worshipper of everything Italian in the '60s and '70s, he could nevertheless see the paradox of that country's situation: Italian design depends on its magazines, which in turn depend for their prestige on Italian design. There being fewer Spanish publications in the field – *ARDI* and *ON Diseño* more or less cover everything, and are still rarely seen abroad – this situation could not arise in Spain. Tusquets believes that there is a strong tradition in Barcelona of comfort and of attention to, and great taste in, detail. There is no doubt that Spain's long tradition of expertise in working wood will continue to thrive, as will those of inlaying in ivory and ebony, and metal craftsmanship – all tremendous advantages for a country that wants its designer furniture to be noticed and desired around Europe.

BD sells through the vast numbers of design shops that thrive around Spain, and through its own outlet BvD in Madrid. The headquarters and a second shop in Barcelona are situated in a building by Lluís Domènech í Montaner and immaculately restored by Estudio Per, winning for BD a top award in 1979. There is now a factory outside each of the two major cities, which among other things produce exact replicas of Gaudí furniture and accessories. In 1987, BD produced a chair called Gaulino (in tribute to Gaudí) designed by Carlos Jane. This was exhibited at La Sala Vinçon, with an abstract sculpture like a fish skeleton made up of

141

elements of the chair. Another, the Coqueta, by Pete Sans, is a finely woven basket-weave scoop seat set on three finely poised aluminium legs, with a leather strap holding it all together.

Another company which combines manufacture with retailing is that of Fernando Amat in Barcelona. Many see Amat as the Spanish Terence Conran, and it is true that he spotted a gap in the home-furnishing market as early as 1973, when he started up. He is a major figure in the design world, some would even call him *el jefe* (the boss). Amat has a single large shop called Galerías Vinçon in Barcelona, where a variety of furniture, furnishings and accessories bought in from around Spain and from other countries is sold. He commissions other designers and has his own manufacturing capacity to produce furniture for his shop as well as for export. He specializes in the area of café and outdoor furniture, for which there is naturally a large demand in Spain, and works on this with some of Spain's top designers. Probably his company's best-known design, and one which epitomizes the quality and creativity of Spanish design, is the aluminium Toledo chair by Jorge Pensi. It is comfortable and beautiful and, they claim, as 'resistant as the fortress of Toledo' which held out against the Republican army for 70 days in 1936 during the Civil War.

Galerías Vinçon has two particular features, the first being a comprehensive selection of design and design-related magazines from all over the world, with a healthy turnover, which gives an idea of the interests of Vinçon's customers. The second is a large exhibition space at the rear of the shop called La Sala Vinçon, where a variety of non-commercial shows takes place. These, on design, art and cultural subjects in the broadest sense of the terms, are often highly experimental in nature, have included performance art and dance and a Minimalist light show activated by the viewer. La Sala Vinçon has been called 'the best design school in the country' by *ARDI* magazine. Major avant-garde art and design movements at home and from abroad have been promoted here, as well as more traditional exhibitions of photography, the fine arts, or celebrations of various events. In true Surrealist tradition, Vinçon sometimes extends its window displays onto the wide pavement – there might be giant teacups, or a flock of cows apparently grazing across it.

Amat lives near Galerías Vinçon in Gaudí's famous Stone Quarry building, in an apartment which confidently and fluently combines the original decorative elements – intricately inlayed floors, elaborate plasterwork and magnificent carved doors – with a collection of his favourite designer furniture. Most of this has been designed especially for use in his flat by the well-known Barcelona designer, Carlos Riart, whose particular preference is for made-to-measure pieces for individual clients. He disdains market research, and designs solely for comfort and convenience, using traditional techniques. The Fernando dining chair has a slight backwards tilt and, more unusually, short arms, both of which are for greater comfort during long Spanish after-dinner debates. For Amat, Riart also designed a long, comfortable sprung sofa, one of his

142

Exterior of Vinçon, Fernando Amat's shop which is the Barcelona (and therefore more fashionable) equivalent of the British Habitat. Crowdpullers have included outsize teacups, and these cows grazing across the wide pavements. Vinçon stocks top designer furniture and accessories, from Spain and elsewhere, as well as an impressive array of international design magazines.

RIGHT *Jorge Pensi's Paris table of 1985 and Toledo chair of 1987 for Amat, the manufacturing arm of Fernando Amat's empire. The revolutionary leg support, besides recalling the Eiffel Tower, provides extra stability.*

Pensi's indomitable Toledo chair for Amat in cast aluminium, named after the town which was beseiged by the Republican army for seventy days during the Civil War, it is extremely strong as well as beautiful.

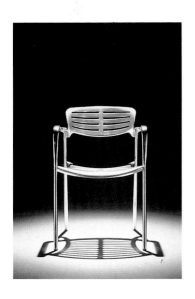

143

FURNITURE

RIGHT *The sensual lines of the practical Lola chair designed by Josep Lluscá for Nova-Norma in 1988, one of a range of office chairs. The arms and legs are in cast aluminium. The seat and back are fully adjustable; as always, Lluscá combines the latest technology with a light, artistic approach.*

OPPOSITE, LEFT *The Naya desk and shelving system, suitable for home use, designed by Josep Lluscá for Enea in 1984. The various elements are totally interchangeable and will easily slot in where required. Wire mesh containers eliminate a build-up of dust. This system won an ADIFAD award in 1986.*

OPPOSITE, RIGHT *The Gigolo clothes hanger for Enea designed by Josep Lluscá in 1986. Surfaces to be in contact with clothes are coated with a non-slip substance; the shoe rack has an especially hardwearing surface. The piece can be folded flat against the wall.*

specialities being solid-looking but shapely upholstered pieces.

Industrial designer Josep Lluscá in Barcelona is also famous for his innovative furniture pieces. Enea, a company manufacturing tubular metal for camping equipment, approached Lluscá to design a camp bed. Lluscá could see other applications of this versatile technique, and the collaboration eventually turned Enea into a designer furniture company of the highest order. One of Lluscá's most comprehensive ranges for Enea, called Naya, consists of adaptable bunk beds, sofa beds, and desk and shelving units. His Gigolo folding clothes hanger, shelving unit and BCN chair, also for Enea, and hallstand for Sellex are simple as well as beautiful and technologically interesting.

Lluscá works on every project personally, with help from his studio. He sees himself as a Rationalist, an admirer of the Bauhaus and of Charles Eames, but the Catalan in him is also drawn irresistibly to Gaudí and the aesthetic functions of organic form. He began his studies in architecture, then went on to industrial design at Eina design school in Barcelona.

Having studied and worked for some time abroad, he returned home to become possibly the most influential Catalan designer in his field. His approach is strictly scientific, and he is passionate about researching the use of new materials and technologies. He is not interested in form for form's sake, but uses sculptural criteria in his designs. His credo is the perfect functioning and serviceability of everyday objects, especially apparent in his product design (see Chapter 6). Comparisons with New York's Morrison Cousins are inevitable. His shapes are Minimalist but elegant, and above all very human – he likes to create works of art with a particular function.

When he first begins work on a new design, he likes to look at all the essentials, and question whether or not they are essential or merely arbitrary. For example, the straight line has been accepted as a necessary element for serial production. But in many modern production methods, the straight line is no easier to achieve than a curve, indeed it can be more difficult, a discovery which has opened up new possibilities for Lluscá.

FURNITURE

His Andrea chair for Andreu Nort in 1988 gave him the opportunity to stretch his imagination with sculptural form as well as producing a chair which was both technologically advanced and comfortable. The shape has definite allusions to Gaudí, as does the use of sculpted wood. Lluscá challenged himself to achieve the look of Gaudí's hand-crafted and polished wood using the new generation of computerized numerical control machines, which produce long series quickly and economically. He was inspired to try using three legs by Charles Eames' ill-fated Side Chair of 1944, which was never produced as it was considered unstable. By inclining the seat – and therefore the weight of the sitter – backwards, widening the space between the legs and shortening the arms to prevent unbalancing the chair when rising up from it he was finally able to achieve stability. The trumpet-shaped support at the back was inspired by chairs of the '50s. The seemingly unlikely combination of all these factors and influences has produced a classic chair for the '90s, one of lasting strength and elegance, owing nothing to the jokey pastiche of post-Modernism.

Javier Mariscal is truly a phenomenon in the design world. He works in virtually every area including fashion, and produces paintings and sculptures as well. His collaboration with the Italian Memphis group in the early '80s brought him personal fame that predated the recognition of Spanish design by the press and design world. Still only in his middle thirties, Mariscal, who is originally from Valencia, is in the thick of the Barcelona design community. His cartoon characters have been used as the mascots of various events and organizations; he has designed graphics and interiors, fabrics and furniture, lighting and even shoes and bed linen.

He is something of an eccentric, seeming to be deliberately provocative or deliberately naïve in his work. He is probably best known for his chair designs, many of which are signed with a graphic flourish on a back or limb, such as his prize-winning Duplex and Single stools of 1981, and his Araña ('spider') lamp of 1985, all for BD. More idiosyncratic are his four chairs for Akaba of 1988: the Tío Pepe (reminiscent of the famous silhouette of the sherry house); the Torera, with bullfighter's cap; the Biscuter, an upholstered motor-scooter shape, and the Garriris, with cartoon mouse ears and feet after his own strip-cartoon character. Mariscal is not particularly strong technically, so he often collaborates with the industrial designer Pepe Cortes; their Trampolin chair with sprung back won them an award in 1986.

Another feminine name, Andrea, for this sculptural chair by Josep Lluscá for Andreu World in 1988. Every line is carved by a computer controlled machine – including the gently rounded back and seat whose organic form was inspired by Gaudí.

The Biscuter, one of many eclectic
chairs by Javier Mariscal for
manufacturers Akaba. The lower
section of the chair is based on a
motor scooter shape, complete with
wheel, whereas the seat and back are
reminiscent of the Trampolin.

Javier Mariscal and Pepe Courets'
Trampolin chair for Akaba of 1986,
which won a prestigious Premio Delta
from ADIFAD in that year. The three
contrasting materials and splash of red
recall the idiom of Memphis at the
time. The Mariscal/Cortes team had
formerly worked for Memphis.

147

FURNITURE

Jorge Pensi, a little older and more sober, came originally from Brazil. Quietly off-beat, he lives and works, with his studio of four designers, in Barcelona's Gothic quarter in preference to the more affluent up-town area favoured by most designers. He is the creator of many well-known successful designs, such as Amat's Toledo chair and, with his former partner Alberto Liévore, upholstered furniture for Perobell. The partnership designed the first exhibition stand for SIDI, whose staunch supporters they have been from the outset.

Pensi prefers to work in a simple idiom, using form itself and the dialogue between form and materials to make his statement. His Paris table for Amat in 1984, which is often paired with the Toledo chair, used a totally revolutionary shape for the legs, both sturdy and elegant. His bookshelf for Disform was purposely made to look solid and heavy, but is actually light and comes packed for self-assembly. In 1989 he designed desk accessories in plexiglass and aluminium for Sabat, and in the same year challenged himself to design a chair made entirely in wood for Andreu Nort, which is industrially produced. A particularly striking piece by Liévore for the company is the red Manolete chair, named after the famous bullfighter. Very upright and taut, it has the suggestion of a hat and its single arm represents the folded arm of the bullfighter holding a cape.

The Horus bed of 1987 designed by Alberto Liévore and Jorge Pensi for Perobell. It is classically simple, but with oblique lines for the legs and bedhead, with a touch of whimsy supplied by a movable bedside table which attaches to the bed.

The Fokker bookcase designed by Jorge Pensi for Disform in 1987. It has been deliberately designed to appear heavy, but is in fact light in structure and can be easily assembled. The upright side sections conceal two small cupboards.

FURNITURE

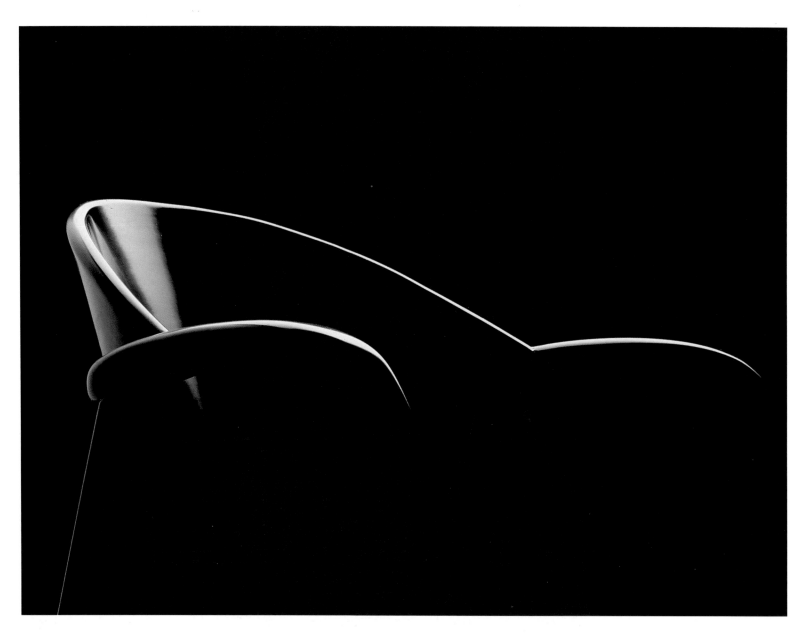

The gently curving lines of Jorge Pensi's Medas chair in wood for Andreu World. With an upholstered seat and firmly positioned legs, this chair is generally used as a conference or dining chair. Pensi keeps tight control of the art direction for photographs of all his work, as this beautifully composed shot suggests.

150

Alberto Liévore's highly dramatic Manolete chair, inspired by the stance of the famous bullfighter of that name, for Perobell, 1988. Its single left arm mimics the arrogant pose, while the blood-red upholstery – the only colour in which it is available – speaks for itself. The taut and upright lines of the chair evoke its spirit effectively in a classic example of how well allusion can work.

151

FURNITURE

Ready to pounce, Pedro Miralles' Lynx chair of 1988 for XO of France. The bend in the front legs gives an unexpected dynamism to what could otherwise be a simple basic chair.

The Madrid architect Pedro Miralles, although still in his early 30s, has already won many awards and scholarships. He is known for his very sympathetic treatment of wood and inlays, but works for many different manufacturers in different materials. His Dry Martini stools for Akaba in 1987 are in the shape of giant cocktail shakers. The double Egipcia lamps for Santa and Cole have the fan shapes of papyrus plants, and are adjustable to form the stylized papyrus shapes seen in ancient Egyptian bas-reliefs. The Andrews Sisters is the cheeky name for a nest of wooden tables he designed for Punt Mobles, with anthropomorphic front feet and a flat support reminiscent of a skirt at the back. A 1989 project for the Italian company Sedie has given him plenty of scope for his imagination. Dining chairs with tall backs 'for increased intimacy and to keep in the delicious odours of food' have an attachment on the back with a terracotta flowerpot augmenting the architectural qualities of the chair as well as allowing the scent of plants to permeate the air.

OPPOSITE, LEFT *Pedro Miralles' imaginative Hakernar dining chair for the Italian company Sedie, of 1989. The plant pots like window boxes give another meaning to the phrase 'architectural furniture'.*

OPPOSITE, RIGHT *More allusions from Pedro Miralles, this time in his Andrews Sisters chairs from Spanish manufacturer Punt Mobles. The presence of the fifties singing troupe is suggested in the shape of legs, and the rear 'train'.*

FURNITURE

MANUFACTURERS

One of the top design-led manufacturers is Punt Mobles. The name is almost synonymous with that name of its managing director and head designer, Vicent Martínez. Born in Valencia, he began his studies there, then went to Massana School in Barcelona. In 1974 he set up his own industrial, graphic and interior design studio, but became frustrated by his inability to find anyone to manufacture his designs. Like a number of designers at the time, this led him to set up his own company with a small manufacturing workshop.

Punt Mobles consists of Martínez, Lola Castello and Francisco Fernández. Their early work was entirely in pine and, having studied north-European markets, they made a brave decision to introduce kit furniture to Spain. As industrial designers they revalued its whole concept, improving the packing, assembly methods and instructions to the customer.

Though you would never guess it from an assembled piece, Punt Mobles still produces furniture which is delivered flat and assembled on site. The sophistication and complexity of some of their pieces make this a surprise and an added delight. In 1984, the launch of a comprehensive range called Concert finally brought the company into the limelight. Angular and Mackintoshian, it has a distinctive raised pattern on the doors. It is a modular range, with an optional glass-fronted cabinet, extra shelving, drawer units and cupboards. In ash-veneered plywood, with different stain finishes, it continues to be a top seller and is exported around the world. It won an award for the best kit furniture at the Valencia Furniture Fair that year.

Another award-winning piece by Punt Mobles is Vicent Martínez' Literatura bookcase of 1985. Using the simple expedient of an additional half-width unit in front which runs on wheels, the bookcase is given half as much shelf-space again using the same wall area. The following year, Martínez' elegant Halley table and Vela bed also won popular acclaim and, like all his pieces, are still in production. Perhaps his most

The elegantly spikey Halley table of 1986 by Vicent Martínez for Punt Mobles. The shape of this small dining table is reminiscent of a lunar landing module, with stabilizing legs.

Vicent Martínez' ingenious Literatura bookcase of 1985, which won an ADIFAD prize in that year. An additional set of shelves runs on wheels in front, almost doubling the capacity of the bookcase without using more wall space. Like all the furniture produced by Martínez' company, Punt Mobles, the bookcase is wooden and can be packed flat.

FURNITURE

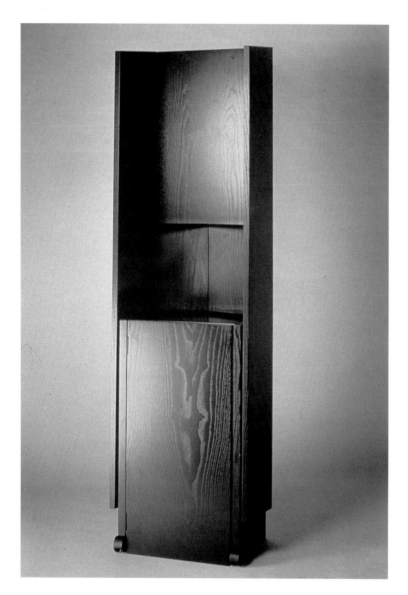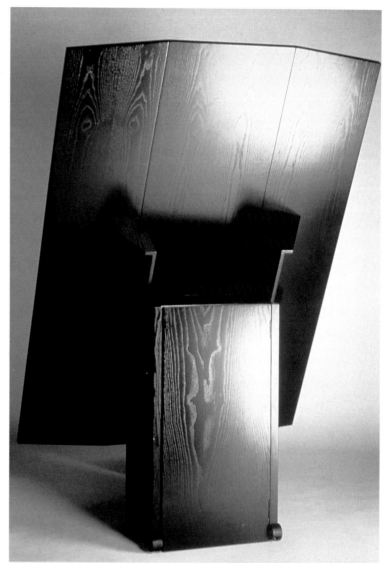

156

spectacular design is that of the Magic table, which could justifiably be classed as an invention. Based on the familiar gate-legged folding table, the Magic table can be folded away with one hand by simply raising one end, which both folds down the flaps and swings the whole surface vertically, forming an elegant shelf-like unit which can stand neatly against a wall using little floor space. This table won a SIDI award for the most popular piece with the public. Continuing an ongoing collaboration with young designers, Punt Mobles has produced pieces by Lola Castello, Vicente Blasco and Pedro Miralles.

Disform (Diseño y Forma) was founded in 1986, first producing household objects but later turning to furniture and accessories. In 1980, the company decided to manufacture nothing but furniture, which had

OPPOSITE, FAR LEFT *Adaptability is an important feature for modern furniture pieces where space is limited. The Magic table by Vicent Martínez for Punt Mobles of 1984 is true to its name. In one form it can be used as a narrow shelving unit.*

OPPOSITE, LEFT *Simply by tipping the back forward, the side sections fold back and the shelving unit begins its transformation. The whole process can be performed with one hand, by means of a strategically placed pivot.*

RIGHT *The Magic table metamorphosed into an elegant dining table in black stained wood. The open door of the 'cupboard' in the lower section acts as a support for the table top.*

FURNITURE

to be competitively priced, easily understood, and folding or with simple assembly. Disform has a reputation for producing pieces which turn into classics. The Subeybaja ('rise and fall') table of 1976 by the Englishman Robert Heritage is still in production today. Its simple but ingenious construction allows it to be used at two heights, for dining or as an occasional table. Disform were the first manufacturers to recognize and put their money behind the French designer Philippe Starck, who is now the undisputed star of the French design firmament. The Len Niggelman armchair of 1986 with its backward tilt and no back legs is one of Starck's best-remembered pieces. The Jon Ild leaning bookcase of 1978, which also has only two legs and supports itself against the wall, is another classic which influenced many other designers. Starck continues to design annual ranges for Disform, who were the first company to succeed in tempting the team of Santiago Miranda and Perry King back to Spain to design a Deco-inspired range for them in 1986.

Artespaña was formed in 1969, part of the Instituto Nacional de Industria (INI), which is the largest industrial holding in the country. The INI originally concentrated on building up Spanish crafts industries by

Another cunningly adaptable table, this time manufactured by Disform and designed by the English furniture designer and former Royal College of Art professor Robert Heritage. A simple adjustment of the folding legs can transform the small dining table into a low coffee table. The Subeybaja (rise and fall) table was designed in 1976 and is still selling.

159

LEFT *The Dabo shelving unit of 1986 designed by Perry King and Santiago Miranda for Disform. This was one of a range in this Deco-inspired style for Disform, and was the first of many to be designed for any Spanish manufacturer by the King and Miranda team, which had settled in Milan.*

Disform was the first manufacturer to spot the potential of the French superstar designer Philippe Starck, who first worked for the company in 1978. This, his Len Niggelman armchair with the strange tilt caused by the lack of back legs, was designed in 1986 and is a best seller. Butter-soft leather and cast aluminium are the materials of this very comfortable chair.

161

supporting the production and marketing of traditional furniture and accessories. There is an interior architecture and decoration department which undertakes projects, including furnishing some of Spain's chain of hotels, the National Paradors. More recently, Artespaña decided to approach some of Spain's top designers to produce an up-market designer furniture range, combining hand processes with contemporary design. This Azimut range was presented at the Milan Furniture Fair in 1988. While worth doing, it was rather an uneven collection with some badly resolved pieces and a confused design philosophy – perhaps some of the designers had not produced their best work for it.

Of the 15 pieces shown, one with true classic potential was Alvaro Soto Aguirre's extending table. The lower part of the legs can be removed to produce a coffee table, and the surface is a square made up of eight veneered triangles. By rotating the table, the four outer triangles can be folded down, making a half-size square table which appears to be covered with a tablecloth; both height and surface area can thus be halved. A pretty marquetry audio-visual cabinet by Oscar Tusquets, an extending TV and video cart by Josep Lluscá and a drawer cabinet by Pedro Miralles were also worthy of note.

Jaime Tressera has also founded his business on craft principles. Using the best materials and handicraft in often highly decorative forms, he sees his furniture as the answer to the aesthetic poverty and brutality of our

OPPOSITE LEFT *Extending table of 1988 by Alvaro Soto Aguirre for Artespaña, the government-backed manufacturing company, here using top designers for the first time in this Azimut collection. By turning the table-top 45 degrees, the hanging leaves can be supported by the legs, doubling the surface area; legs are adjustable in length.*

OPPOSITE RIGHT *Josep Lluscá's Sarda TV and video trolley for Artespaña of 1988. It can be adjusted to fit any size. The walnut veneer is a new departure for Lluscá.*

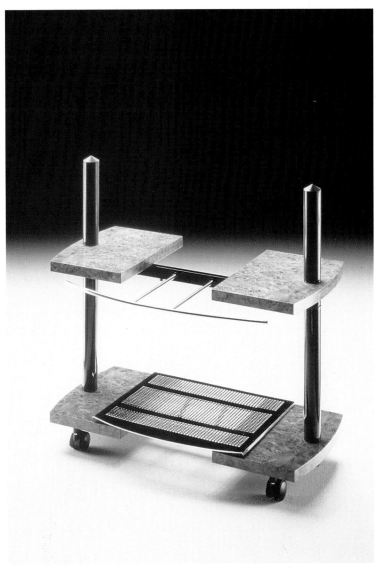

FURNITURE

industrial age. Walnut veneer in different finishes with marquetry inlays are the company trademark. He also uses brass treated in a variety of ways to give a range of finishes. Velvet and leathers are used exclusively for upholstery.

Tressera originally intended to make a career in law, but left that to study jewellery design at Massana in Barcelona. He then spent some years in advertising before beginning to design interiors and architecture, which led him naturally to furniture and lighting design. His aptly named Butterfly desk, Contrapunto bookshelves and inlaid screens are his best-known and most remarkable work, and he has won many awards. His pieces are characterized by a distinctive use of decoration and a delicacy of form – qualities that are comparatively unusual in contemporary furniture design.

The beautifully executed Butterfly writing desk of 1988 by Jaime Tressera, manufactured by his own company. The wings are here shown raised to allow access to a variety of drawers and compartments.

Inlaid wooden screen by Jaime
Tressera, 1988. Traditional craftsman
techniques and careful choice of woods
are essential to this decorative style.

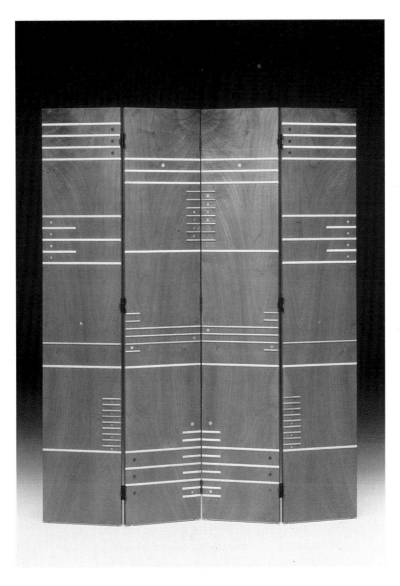

FURNITURE

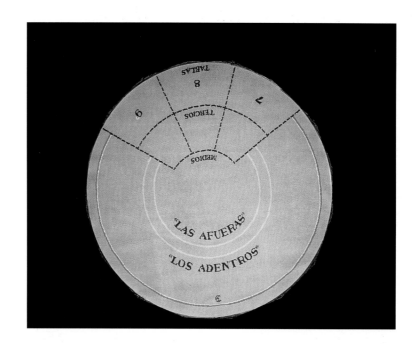

A plan of the bullring showing the traditional divisions has been converted into a rug for Nani Marquina, designed by Eduardo Samsó. It is called A las Cinco de la Tarde (5 o'clock) – the hour of the corrida.

OPPOSITE The Perspectiva rug for Nani Marquina designed by Rafael Marquina. A very traditional country house drawn in perspective has an unlikely Persian carpet instead of a front lawn.

TEXTILES

Carpets and rugs by well-known designers are produced by a company run by and named after the textile designer Nani Marquina in Barcelona. Apart from producing many of her own designs, Marquina has commissioned top designers such as Jorge Pensi and Eduardo Samsó. Many of them make use of the favourite type of Spanish humour, irony. Work by Javier Mariscal includes León Solitario ('Lonely Lion'), a deep blue rug with flowery border and a single caricature lion roaming across it. Mariscal's Estambul rug is inspired by oriental patterns, but is executed like a rough pencil sketch of an original design. Rafael Marquina's Perspectiva rug has woven into it a perspective drawing of a grand mansion with an avenue of trees, and an unlikely looking patterned rug on the lawn. Architect Eduardo Samsó's A Las 5 de la Tarde ('5 p.m.') is circular and sand-coloured, with a plan of a bullring woven into it, 'the drawing-room carpet for genuine lovers of the bullfight'. Nani Marquina produces witty and well-made rugs for domestic and office environments, and exports successfully around the world, making use of the expertise of small workshops to manufacture short-run specialist products.

FURNITURE

ABOVE AND LEFT *Wild lively patterns by Javier Mariscal, with motives of fighting cocks, plants and flowers. These designs for the manufacturer Marieta have been used for upholstery fabrics; others by Mariscal are used for shower curtains, bedlinen and rugs.*

Spanish upholstery fabrics have a world-wide reputation for quality. Isabel García Tapia runs her own company producing fabrics and fabric wall coverings which combine traditional aesthetics and modern techniques. She often copies fragments of antique fabrics, especially ecclesiastical robes, for their richness and colouring. She has been responsible for many collaborations with architects on restoration projects, producing the closest possible match to original fabric compositions. At other times she will alter an original wallpaper design for use as curtain, upholstery fabric and wall-covering patterns. But she also produces bright modern designs which are bold but never too striking, tending towards North African patterns and colours. One of her most important features is texture, and she uses this to great effect when called upon to design an interior in traditional Spanish style.

Catering for a different end of the market, Marieta manufactures upholstery fabrics and carpets by top designers, architects and artists. For many years the company has had a collaboration with Javier Mariscal which has produced a large range of bed linen, curtain and upholstery fabric, carpets and even shower curtains in hot African colours that work well in Spain.

169

FURNITURE

PRODUCT DESIGN

If we continue using design as practical magic, the market will leave us in the corner, a pathetic image of an adversary cowering, awaiting the next assault. We dream of full moons reclined on a Memphis sofa.

(ALBERTO CORAZÓN, *DISEÑO EN ESPAÑA*, MINISTRY OF INDUSTRY AND ENERGY, 1985)

The Fenix hanging light designed by Jorge García Garay for his company, García Garay, in 1988. Allusions to the phoenix, with references to flight and light, are made with its wing-like reflectors. This light was chosen for the inaugural exhibition at London's Design Museum in 1989.

The beginning of industrial organization in Spain can be traced back to the early eighteenth century, the time of the first Bourbon king, Philip V. With Europe constantly at war and trade restrictions or heavy taxes common, the court and nobility could no longer import the luxury items they were accustomed to. To solve this problem, the imaginative king set up the first Real Fabrica (Royal Factory) at the Escorial, where the best artisans, Spanish or from other parts of Europe, worked under one roof to produce the fine objects their employers demanded. A network of these factories, specializing in different crafts, was set up in various regions of Spain, and artists were brought in from all over Europe to teach special techniques. Nearly all the output consisted of convincing copies of items from abroad, partly because this was what the new foreign rulers and their court wanted, and partly because there was no sufficiently strong Spanish vernacular style of decoration and design at this time. The Reales Fabricas continued to flourish in Spain up to the Peninsular War, when some were deliberately destroyed and others were bought and continued under different management, still carrying their former names. The last Real Fabrica closed its doors in 1850.

The example of the Wedgwood factory in England, set up in 1769, was copied throughout Europe, especially in Spain. It epitomized the meeting of Classical art and industry predominant at that period, when Classical friezes were frequently applied to domestic products. Engravers and artists, whose status suddenly increased, were dispatched to Italy to copy Classical designs which were then adapted for use on china, fabrics, wall coverings and even packaging. The importance of formal art

171

training, particularly drawing skills, was recognized by the Barcelona administration setting up the Escuela Gratuita de Diseño ('Free Design School') in 1775. This was funded by local industry with the specific aim of teaching drawing skills to improve the standard of prints for the region's most virile industry, textile weaving and printing, most particularly of their specialist printed calicos or *indianas* which were exported around Europe. In 1789 Charles IV went so far as to demand by royal decree that all apprentices and guild workers must learn to draw – though this was never put into practice.

The upheaval and sufferings of the Peninsular War were over in 1814, and despite the number of constitutional crises between then and the end of the century, all the major industrial centres around Spain – Bilbao, San Sebastián, Valencia, Barcelona and Madrid – saw a period of tremendous growth. This was a time when skirts would use up to ten metres of fabric, a fashion that reached its peak in 1860, but unhappily for the Catalan textile producers it coincided with a period of violent regionalist activities. To punish the Catalans, Madrid raised taxes on raw materials and kept taxes on imported goods low, causing many textile manufacturers to fight for survival while others turned their production towards light-industrial consumer goods, with a high turnover and a ready market.

Regular national exhibitions celebrating industry were held in the second half of the nineteenth century, with an emphasis on applied art and furniture. A Spanish presence at international exhibitions was rare, but this situation was rectified by Spain's own contribution, the Universal Exhibition at Barcelona in 1888. Many craftsmen and designers, displeased at seeing the large number of copies and poor reproductions they saw there, began to reject imitation and mass production and turn towards the principles of John Ruskin and William Morris. There was a strong movement for a return to old standards of hand craftsmanship, which assured the success of the similarly committed architects Lluís Domènech í Montaner and Antoni Gaudí.

But because of the long industrial tradition of Catalonia, designers were inevitably drawn to a middle path, where industrial techniques could be adapted to create artistic objects, often happily. This was the case with the regional speciality of tile production: many of the leading designers of the period, including Gaudí and Domènech í Montaner, worked successfully using a mixture of hand craftsmanship and cleverly adapted production methods. Variations on this philosophy continued, eventually clashing with the Industrial Aesthetic of Le Corbusier, which rejected traditional skills. Spanish supporters of this new aesthetic, inspired by the work of Mies van der Rohe for the Barcelona International Exhibition of 1929, founded in 1930 an organization called GATPAC (Grup Català d'Arquitectes i Tecnics per a la Soluciò dels Problemes de l'Arquitectura Contemporania), and subsequently a school on Bauhaus principles in 1936.

Franco's victory in 1939 put an end to Spain's participation in the international design scene. Catalonia suffered particularly, indeed, the

The silver tea set designed by Oscar Tusquets in 1980 for Italian manufacturer Alessi. Famous for commissioning top international architects to produce domestic objects – the Michael Graves Alessi kettle, the Ettore Sottsass coffee set – Alessi was the first company to recognise Spanish design talent in this way. The organic shapes are typical of Tusquets.

173

PRODUCT DESIGN

practice of industrial design was actually prohibited: it was seen as a form of culture, and all cultural activities in Catalonia were expressly forbidden. This meant that nearly all activity in the field of industrial design for the following 20 years was conducted either clandestinely or vicariously, through foreign design magazines. Restrictions began to loosen during the '50s (Spain opened its doors to selective trade in 1951) but organizations still had to be set up with great tact and cunning so as not to excite the interest of central government. One early industrial design association, IDIB (Instituto de Diseño Industrial de Barcelona), was eventually banned.

ADVANCES IN INDUSTRIAL DESIGN

So much building was done during the boom years of the early '60s that industry had to be allowed to develop. In this period André Ricard, who began his career in the late '50s and was for many years a prime force and a national representative of Spanish industrial design abroad, designed and produced domestic accessories, some using the new plastic moulding techniques, whose like had previously been seen only in Italy and Britain. In 1960 he, Antoni de Moragas Gallissà and Alexandre Cirici founded ADIFAD, the industrial design branch of FAD (Fomento de las Artes Decorativas), and the following year they were able to award the Premios Delta prizes for industrial design for the first time. Lack of investment in the field meant that juries could find themselves awarding prizes for more or less experimental objects, but this situation improved due to the existence of ADIFAD and a healthier economy. In 1967, BCD (Barcelona Centro de Diseño), a coordinating body for design organizations, was founded, at last giving design the face of authority it needed.

Ricard, French but born in Barcelona in the year of the International Exhibition, was for some time regarded as a controversial figure and something of an agitator, but he is now highly respected. Having worked on the ICSID (International Congress of Societies of Industrial Design) study group in the early '60s, he then allied it and ADIFAD, forming the international platform that Spanish designers needed in order to gain respect from their peers and keep up to date with European design affairs. It was a tremendously exciting period for Spanish designers; Ricard calls it a 'Golden Age'. Ideological similarities with other European designers and differences with many US designer/stylists could now be identified and discussed. Ricard became a friend of that great US industrial designer/stylist Raymond Loewy, beginning an association which continued for years. Experimentation with new materials and techniques was at its height, with moulded plastics at the forefront.

Ricard's personal contribution included some seminal work, including the revolutionary ice tongs of 1964 made from one single strip of plastic and the Copenhagen stacking ashtrays of 1966. He has won innumerable prizes for packaging and domestic objects, as well as being in charge of

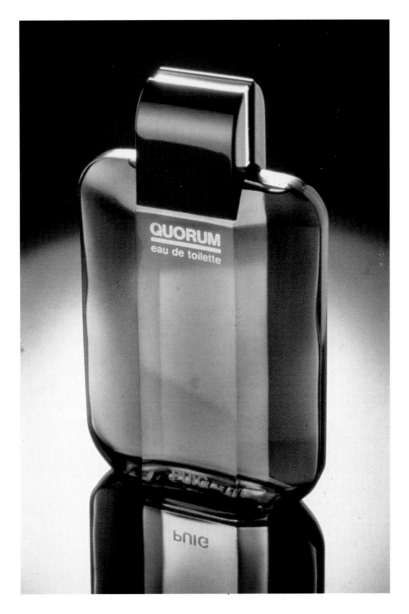

André Ricard's classic design for the packaging of Quorum eau de toilette for Puig, 1984. Ricard is one of the founding fathers of modern Spanish design, and has worked in many different disciplines. His Quorum packaging is one of the great Spanish classics of its genre.

PRODUCT DESIGN

Another classic, this time of the sixties, and forerunner of many other similiar lamps, Miguel Milá's TMC light of 1961. Its utter simplicity is balanced by a clever device in the handle, which will lower or heighten the light by use of a lock-releasing grip. This lamp also won a special ADIFAD Delta de Oro award commemorating 25 years of the organization.

ABOVE *Essential to the Spanish breakfast of freshly squeezed orange juice, this juice extractor designed by André Ricard has been manufactured by Moulinex.*

BELOW *Ricard's white composite kitchen sink of 1988 for Sangra was another ADIFAD prize-winning design.*

the design concepts behind the recently refurbished Centro de Arte Reina Sofía in Madrid. His famous design for Quorum *eau de toilette* for Puig in 1984 has appeared in many 'best of' design surveys, as has his bottle for La Nuit for Paco Rabanne. In 1985 he designed a dossier in the form of a small folding filing cabinet for the 'Barcelona 1992' presentation to the International Olympic Committee. Kitchen sinks, china and juice extractors have all come under Ricard's eye; he designed the ingenious Moulinex rechargeable mixer/blender in 1987.

A contemporary and sometime collaborator of Ricard is Miguel Milá Sagnier, who trained in Barcelona as an architect, working in industrial design and interiors since the late '50s. One of the first ADIFAD prizes went to his TMC floor lamp of 1961, whose height can be adjusted by gripping a handle attached to the light. The Caracol ('snail') spiral staircase of 1975 has teak steps cleverly designed with little apparent means of support. Another ADIFAD winner is his well-publicized Ximenea free-standing fireplace of 1977. A new version of this popular design, the Mesina, was produced in 1989. Door furniture and office accessories are among his other accomplishments, and in 1986 he redesigned Barcelona's Metro system and trains.

Milá's fireplaces and the Caracol staircase were both produced by manufacturers DAE (Diseño Ahorro Energetico, 'Energy-Saving Design'). DAE was set up specifically to research and produce commercially all kinds of energy-saving designs for the domestic and contract market. Solar energy is a particular interest. This forward-thinking company commissions the country's top designers, such as Oriol Bohigas, the team of Ramón Isern and Gemma Bernal, Oscar Tusquets, Pep Bonet, Lluís Clotet, Federico Correa and David Mackay.

A combination of Gaudí and Charles Eames may not be an obvious route to the design of a pressure cooker, but this is the one taken by Josep Lluscá responding to the deliberately anthropomorphic shapes of the New York industrial designer Morrison Cousins. Lluscá produces designs which are both totally functional and pleasant to use: 'no visual pollution' is his maxim. His Splendid pressure cooker of 1986 for Fagor is revolutionary as well as handsome to behold. To make production cheaper and more efficient, and assembly easier, all the mechanisms are housed in the handle, formed of pure-plastic components which clip together without screws. Handle, handle release, pressure gauge and a weight to replace the valve have been completely redesigned, making them easier both to understand and to use. A new method of gaining pressure saves nearly three-quarters of the energy and is three times quicker than the conventional system. Using a device less alarming to the user than conventional, steam-whistling pressure cookers, Lluscá's circle of dots is designed to rotate, turning by optical illusion into a white circle when the correct pressure has been reached.

Lluscá's best-known light, the Bolonia bedside table lamp, was designed for Metalarte in 1987, its shape borrowed from the traditional bedside water bottle with a little upturned glass acting as the cork. The lamp has two qualities of light: the base of translucent glass can glow softly for a diffused light, but for a shaft of light for reading the articulated top can be raised revealing the halogen bulb. His Anade table lamp designed in 1984, also for Metalarte, has an infinitely adjustable arm with a head which pivots so that it is always pointing downwards. His Gavina ceiling lamp and Saeta floor lamp, both for Blauet in 1987, are so minimal they are barely there at all – just thin strips of steel and tiny halogen lights.

Lluscá's other areas of work include bath accessories, door furniture for Sellex, packaging and computers, and he also does much experimental design on his own behalf, his clients being too conservative to fund him for this. One such project is a revolutionary mechanism for a fridge door which allows it to be adjusted quite easily to open on either the right or the left. He is also experimenting with possible new uses of carbon fibre compound. Lluscá, who has won many awards and whose work has been exhibited around Europe, is realistic but hopeful about Spanish manufacturing companies. Many have become so accustomed to copying foreign goods that they have little confidence in the viability of commissioning new designs, but the success of Lluscá's modern classics, which are long-lasting, elegant and do not date, might convince them in the near future.

DESIGNERS AND MANUFACTURERS

Oscar Tusquets' manufacturing company, BD (Barcelona Diseño), produces his own and other designers' lights and products. Tusquets' Bib Luz ('library light') of 1985, made to fit a range of BD shelving, is in the shape of a book, with an aluminium shell holding the transformer and switch. From this 'book' a halogen light is suspended by an adjustable curving rod which can light up any section of the bookcase, and there is a detachable plug which connects with wiring passed through hollow sections in the shelves. A variation of this light designed in the same year can be used either as a table or as a wall-mounted light. BD produces many types of shelving, some of which have no visible means of fixing, and others which have invisible light sources.

Door furniture by a variety of designers, bathroom accessories and even letterboxes for blocks of flats are also designed for manufacture by BD. Tusquets has commissioned top designers such as Miguel Milá, André Ricard, Javier Mariscal, Antoni de Moragas – indeed most of the major figures in Spanish design – plus some from abroad such as Italians Ettore Sottsass and Alessandro Mendini, Portuguese Alvaro Siza and American Robert Stern. The firm has won many awards including a coveted Gold from ADIFAD in the special 25th-anniversary prizes in 1987. This was given for the Hialina shelving system by Lluís Clotet, Tusquets and Oriol Bohigas. Since 1987, Tusquets himself has been concentrating more on architectural projects, with his partner Carlos Diaz.

Quod was set up in 1983, and has departments covering industrial,

The design for the Barcelona metro by Miguel Milá, 1986.

Miguel Milá's Caracol (snail) staircase, for manufacturers DAE in 1975 won an ADIFAD award in that year.

Miguel Milá's door furniture for DAE.

PRODUCT DESIGN

graphic and environmental design. Much of their work comes from the local government, and this is increasing as 1992 approaches. Other work comes from large multinational companies such as Black and Decker, Land Rover, SEAT and Fagor. This is bottom-line industrial design; experimental or avant-garde work is not relevant, as the clients are extremely conservative. They are often most concerned with updating or restyling to gain a foothold in the Spanish market. As fees are paid on a royalty basis, Quod is not tempted to push out the boundaries of acceptability, and is often unfairly accused of being unimaginative.

Capdevila and Associates is run by Guillermo Capdevila, who graduated from the Royal College of Art in London in 1975. The company works frequently for Solac, the rival of Fagor, and in fact comprises Solac's only design input. Capdevila's cordless iron, first produced in 1985, was designed to change buying patterns, and it is typical of the Spanish domestic consumer market that it was produced and marketed with very little preliminary research. Solac was determined to get it onto the market first, come what may, and develop it according to public response, which meant that, in an effort to keep one step ahead of their competitors, more advanced versions were brought out effectively in competition with earlier ones. This rather cavalier attitude did at least give a boost to the previously static iron market by drawing attention to this essential but unadventurous domestic item.

The Valencian design consultancy La Nave is fortunate to number among its staff industrial designer Daniel Nebot, who often collaborates with Nacho Lavernia. Among Nebot's award-winning designs are signing systems and a range of car roof-racks, while the Nebot and Lavernia collaboration was responsible for an elegant electric heater and an important public water fountain for Industrias Saludes.

Transatlantic, an industrial design consultancy based in Barcelona since 1983, also produces many furniture designs, as is common in Spain. The partners are Lluís Morillas, Josep Puig and Ramón Benedito. They work on totally experimental projects, such as Muebles Transcendentes ('Transcendental Furniture'), and rather risqué pieces such as their award-winning Frenesí stool of 1986 which sports an unmistakably phallic limb. Benedito also works in highly specialized high-technology areas, normally the preserve of engineers, such as loudspeakers for music systems, and weighing machines for the medical world.

Like Josep Lluscá, Jorge Garciá Garay, who originated from Buenos Aires but found cultural links with the Catalans and settled in Barcelona, has been influenced by the Rationalist movement. He has been designing and manufacturing lighting, and occasionally furniture, since the late '70s, and has now turned exclusively to lighting, for which he uses the usual Spanish design language for this product, which is Minimalist. Simple detailing, close relation between form and function and economy of manufacture are all essential to his way of thinking. He and Lluscà championed the use of dichroic and halogen lights in Spain, and are generally considered to be leaders in this field. Garay has recently begun to produce lights which change their appearance in some way when

The Bolonia bedside lamp by Josep Lluscá for Metalarte in 1986. The shape is taken from the classic water vase and upturned glass traditionally placed on bedside tables. The top can be lifted to reveal a tiny halogen spotlight for bedtime reading.

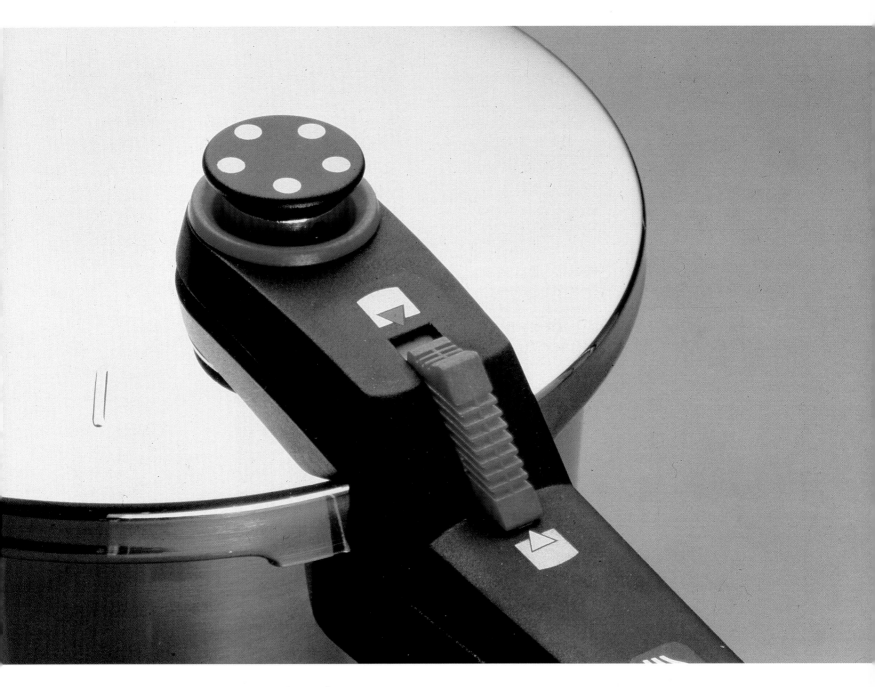

Josep Lluscá's magnificent pressure cooker, the Splendid, for Fagor of 1986. All the components are plastic and housed in the handle; they clip together rather than using screws, for economy and ease of assembly.

181

PRODUCT DESIGN

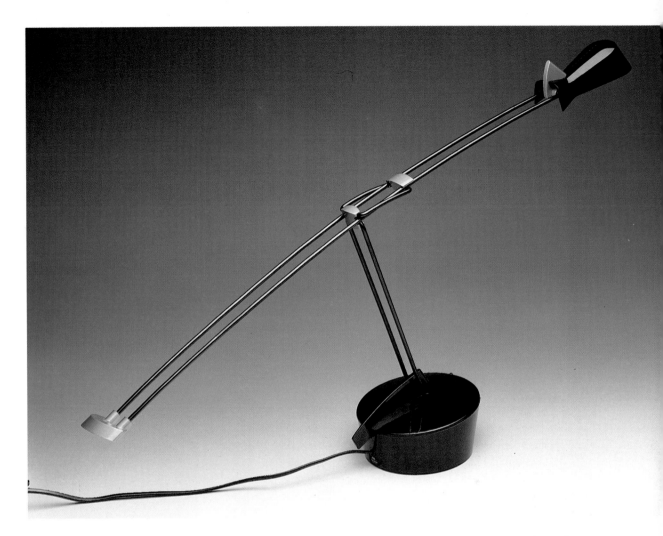

Fruit of a collaboration between Josep Lluscá and jewellery designer Joaquín Berao, the Ketupa table lamp for Metalarte is a beautifully resolved piece of architecture.

illuminated, either taking on an unexpected spectrum of colours or tones, or seeming to change shape altogether. Originally he favoured hand-craft methods, but since the early '80s has turned to industrial production. Past collaborations have been with Miguel Milá and with the team of Ramón Isern and Gemma Bernal, though most recently he has designed most of his factory's output himself.

Garay's Pitagoras ('Pythagoras') lamp of 1983 was the beginning of a successful floor-lamp range. Consisting of a simple black vertical pole crossed diagonally by another which holds the light and shade, the Pitagoras is timeless and has proved a considerable commercial success. There are two other lights in the range: the Sputnik, which is adjustable by means of balancing the arm against three alternative catches through a Sputnik-like ball, and the award-winning Pescador ('Fisherman'), whose light dangles languorously from the end of an upright shaped like a fishing rod.

His Altair range of 1986 features a ceiling lamp with a horizontally suspended circle lit by two dichroic lights. These are on hinged brackets which can be swung round to uplight or downlight the reflector depending on the level of light required. The Enterprise floor and ceiling lamp is reminiscent of a propeller, with uplights pointing at curved white reflectors. Perhaps the most dramatic range is his Fenix ('Phoenix') ceiling, wall and floor lamps, which again use the principle of reflected light but with curved reflectors forming the shape of a bird in flight. The Enterprise and Fenix ranges were selected to be shown at the inaugural exhibition of the Design Museum in London in June 1989.

Jorge Pensi, another Argentinian exile, has produced many designs for Belux, the best-known being those in polished cast aluminium, a rather cool and aloof material which he uses in gentle curving shapes, both architectural and sculptural. His Regina range, based on a simple triangular lampshade shape, comprises a wall-mounted uplighter, a floor-standing version and ceiling and desk lights which are ingeniously adjustable in height by seemingly invisible means. There are similar variations in the Olympia range, but the shade for each version is in the shape of a long bean. Pensi's Taps light, either desk or floor standing, is

PRODUCT DESIGN

rather friendlier, with a tiny adjustable shade shaped like a nun's wimple.

Apart from his extensive work in the fields of furniture and lighting, Pensi has designed products for the Barcelona company Kendal, including a hairdrier, electric radiators and a solar-heated shower. He has advised Amat Furniture on new manufacturing processes, and proposed developments both for the velvet industry and for Granada's furniture industry.

The team of Josep Massana and Josep Tremoleda were among the first to graduate (in 1969) from the new industrial design section at Escuela Massana in Barcelona. Their partnership dated from that time, consolidating in 1973 with the appearance of their shop, interiors and manufacturing business, called Mobles 114. They produce lighting, furniture and accessories mainly to their own designs. One of their lights, the Gira, a compact table lamp, has become a classic of all time. First produced in 1978, it has had steady sales ever since with no redesigning necessary, indeed it is so ageless that it has been publicized as a new product by journalists seeing it for the first time. Sitting on a small square base which is also the axis of the upright, the lamp has a little triangular shade which can be tilted. As a reading light it is functional and undemanding; it is economical with space as it has no angled upright, and it also has a friendly appeal. The base is cast iron, and the shade is aluminium, either anodized or painted to match the base.

Spain's top lighting companies are as inspired and adventurous as the furniture producers, and often work with them and exhibit alongside them at trade fairs. Some lighting companies also produce furniture, and some furniture companies also produce lighting. Many of these firms are consolidating their position in the home market before launching themselves into the international one, while some are already exporting about a third of their output.

Oscar Tusquets' amusing library lamp, the Bib Luz, of 1985 for his company BD Ediciones de Diseño. The book-shaped lamp clips onto a special track and does not need individual wiring, so that it can be moved around to light any section of the bookshelves, which are also designed by Tusquets. Photo by Lluís Casals.

Using light reflected off semi-circular wings for shades, the Enterprise ceiling light by Jorge García Garay for García Garay is a striking piece of technology.

Water fountain with obvious allusions to waves in the handle, designed by Daniel Nebot and Nacho Lavernia of La Nave design group for Industrias Saludes.

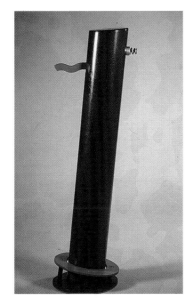

185

PRODUCT DESIGN

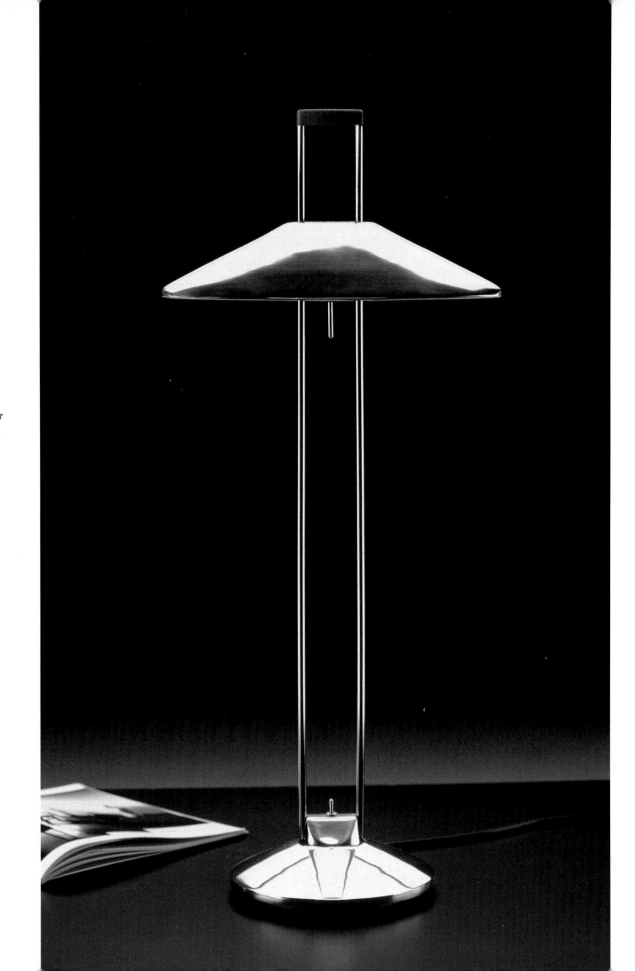

Jorge Pensi's timeless Regina lamp for Belux, 1987, in polished aluminium.

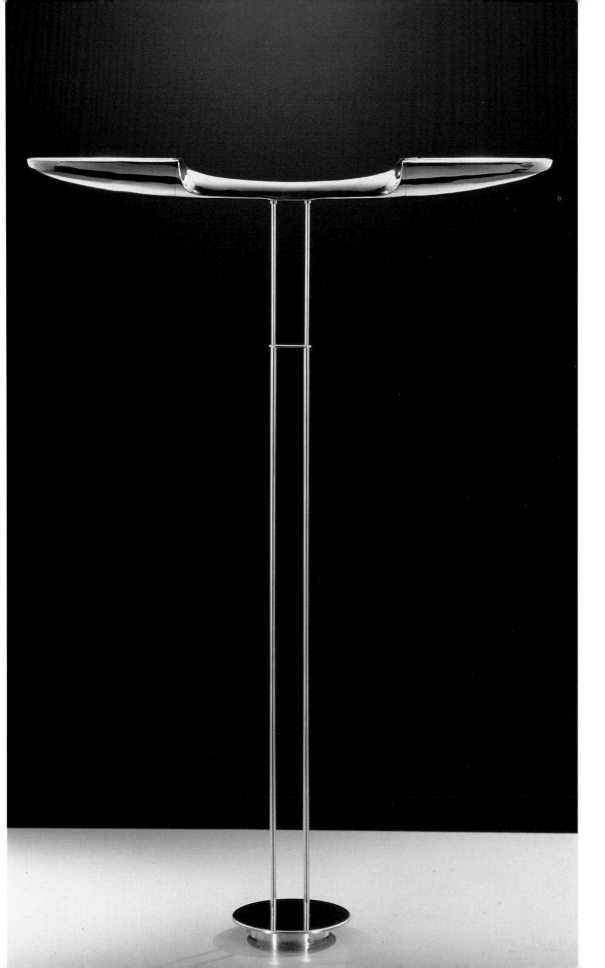

The Olympia ceiling light for Belux by Jorge Pensi, 1988.

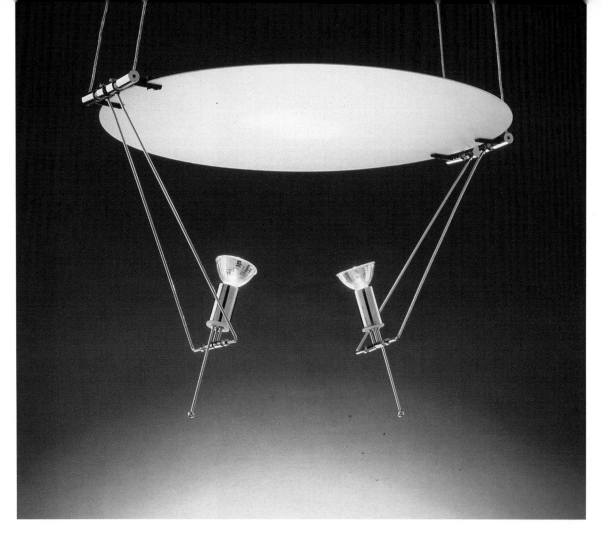

García Garay's extraordinary Altair
ceiling light of 1986.

Another link the lighting and furniture companies have in common is the thin (or non-existent) line between domestic and contract pieces, which tends to benefit both offices and homes. A leading firm is Metalarte, which works with some of the foremost designers in Spain, André Ricard, Josep Lluscá, Enric Franch, Estudi Blanch and Sergi Devesa among them. Lluscá's Bolonia light is destined to become a classic: its witty counterpoint between high-tech function and everyday, familiar appearance typifies the new generation of Spanish product design in which purpose is appealingly combined with a sense of fun. In a similar spirit, Xavier Sole's Arca ceiling light of 1988 is a play on geometry, based on four triangles. One is the ceiling fitting, while the next two are formed by two wires joined at a certain point, supporting a solid base from which is suspended the fourth triangle, a tiny lampshade. A simply executed shape, but one with endless fascination.

In the same year Joan Auge designed a range of lights for Taller Uno. Auge's lights, strangely solid and sculptural beside the more common Minimalist ones, neither borrow shapes nor make clear allusions; in fact, they have a slightly Art Deco flavour. His Thema table lamp is virtually two-dimensional, with a long narrow base and two parallel short uprights supporting a long, narrow, curved translucent blue-glass shade. His Club table lamp has an anodized base and matching larger shade, with an interior feature of a large illuminated frosted bowl. His Alien wall lamp has a curved sliver of polished aluminium supporting a circular frosted diffuser shade.

The best-selling Gira table lamp of
1978 by Josep Massana and Josep
Tremoleda, manufactured by their
own company, Mobles 114. The
slightly kitsch shape with unusual
placing of a pivot is a typically
Spanish play on traditions.

The Taps table lamp by Jorge Pensi for
Belux, 1988, has a shade like a nun's
cowl, adjustable by moving a tiny
handle.

189

PRODUCT DESIGN

*Xavier Soler's cheeky Arca ceiling light
for Metalarte.*

The chic and very restrained Egipcia lamps by Pedro Miralles for Santa and Cole. Taking their shape from papyrus flowers, the uprights branch out and are adjustable, giving the shape of papyrus in its natural state.

The deliberately suggestive Frenesí (frenzy) bar stool by product design team Transatlantic. Winner of an ADIFAD award in 1987.

URBAN DESIGN

Another growing market in Spain, since the massive urban renewal programmes were put into force around the country, is street furniture. This is another of Josep Lluscá's fields. Discussing design of some bus stops, he says that he likes to design 'a little bit of architecture, not furniture for the street'. Using materials which weather well, he particularly likes to use wood components, as he claims that wood 'looks good with writing and graffiti'.

In Barcelona, Santiago Miranda, whose furniture borders on sculpture, has designed overhead supports for traffic lights. Artists and designers alike have been asked to produce designs for water fountains for the vast numbers of squares and public meeting places which have been or are being created. Other administrations around the country are working on similar projects – indeed, the number of new and finely designed fountains alone must reach thousands. A high level of artistry is seen in various new types of paving tiles or iron grates around both fountains and newly planted trees, as well as in park benches, balustrades and street or park lights. Bus stops, signing and even street newspaper kiosks are being designed by the country's top practitioners.

All this is evidence that Spain is laying the foundation of a strong public design heritage. But as Alberto Corazón's comment at the beginning of this chapter implies, there is reason to believe that the value of good product design is underestimated in Spain. This is hardly surprising, since for 20 years in the very recent past the practice of product design was actually prohibited, and product design courses have only existed for a couple of decades at most. Even today many product designers are people who have been trained in very different areas, and much industrial design is the work of engineers, who have not been trained to combine functionalism with aesthetics.

Some designers have been employed for consultancy work with manufacturers under a government-run scheme which paid fees to encourage serious use of design. But many of the projects have not been completed, nor have suggestions been put into force – many manufacturers do not understand the full value of fully trained industrial designers or the scope of their work. As many international companies are setting up in Spain, Ford and Sanyo among them, Spain will either have to rethink its policy on product and industrial design or see its major national industries peak and eventually decline. Spain is not, of course, the only European country facing this challenge, and education can be a long-term solution. As Pere Aguirre, director general of BCD, says in *El Diseño en España* (Ministry of Industry and Energy, 1985), 'Let us value objects of total not partial design, whose integration of all factors constitutes the final result.'

PLANNING THE FUTURE

'*The New Spain returns to her past, using the best of her traditions to build the future – a free, plural and tolerant Spain . . .* '

(HM KING JUAN CARLOS OF SPAIN, 1986)

The forward-thinking Spaniards are using the epoch-making year of 1992 to reorganize their country's infrastructure. New or enlarged airports, road networks and railways will be connecting rural areas with major cities – to the benefit of both, as the less well-known outlying regions will become more accessible. Exhaustive and far-reaching plans for urban refurbishment, relocation of industrial centres and massive building projects are under way to cater for the tens of millions of visitors expected in Olympics year. But 1992 is not to be only a time of celebrating the new face of Spain, and drawing the world's attention to its attractions: every peseta spent is seen as an investment in the future of a country undergoing a rapid transition to meet – or to be one step ahead of — the demands of the twenty-first century. Major government investment is encouraging Madrid to establish itself as an area for high-technology industries, while major national and international communications companies are setting up in Seville and Barcelona in readiness to transmit the events of 1992 by satellite around the world.

SEVILLE

Seville is the capital of the largest region in Spain, with the biggest population. Andalucía's wealth comes from fruit plantations, olive groves and vineyards, the great sherry *bodegas* of Jerez de la Frontera, and the bustling Costa del Sol, besieged every year by French, German and English tourists. But nowadays shipbuilding and petrochemicals, lead and

The restored main entrance facade to the Barcelona Olympic stadium by Federico Correa. Set in what was previously an almost derelict park, the stadium is now surrounded by newly landscaped gardens, piazzas, walkways and steps.

193

Poster showing an aerial plan of the World Expo site in Seville. The new lake ringed with international pavilions is clearly seen, as is the formerly dry ox-bow of the river to the left. El Recinto de la Cartuja is to the rear of the site, reached by the monorail which snakes around it from the amusement park, front right.

TOP RIGHT *The logo for the Seville World Expo, which is being used on all literature and products.*

copper mining, aircraft manufacture, shipping and stainless-steel manufacture also play a major role in what may once have been, but is certainly not now, the sleepy south of Spain. Certainly, the 1992 Universal Exposition held in Seville will focus world attention on the region's resources.

Unlike Madrid and Barcelona, Seville is not the main tourist attraction of its region. This historic city with its countless Moorish buildings, its medieval quarter with authentic flamenco bars hidden down tiny winding streets, hordes of begging gypsies, and ancient religious shrines with bizarre rituals, has a very special quality which has to be sought out and may not appeal to the average tourist. The region, with its vast and inhospitable mountain ranges, is largely composed of tiny villages where the click of Japanese cameras is rarely heard. It is both beautiful and inaccessible, with many hidden treasures known only to the initiated. In one village, for instance, a young boy is keeper of a huge iron key, which unlocks an unremarkable door to an upper room in a country church – revealing a little-known collection of paintings by Francisco de Zurbarán. In parts of Granada and Cadiz, traditions die hard. Many of the huge shuttered mansions lining Las Palmeras in Seville are bastions of Old Spain, where Franco is deeply mourned, the servants still wear white gloves, and the events of 1992 are anticipated with horror.

The area to be developed for the Universal Exposition is part of an historic island in the Guadalquivir river, comprising some 430 hectares. Though very close to the centre of the city, the island, El Recinto de la Cartuja, has been disused for years. It is the site of a very ancient monastery, from which it takes its name. Its oldest building is an eleventh-century domed chapel built to commemorate a vision of the Holy Virgin, but it continued as a religious site for centuries. Christopher Columbus had a special feeling for La Cartuja, and when he ceased travelling lived there for many years, developing his ideas on astronomy and navigation with the monks. He was buried in the monastery chapel – though his remains were moved at a later date – and an ancient baobab tree in the grounds is reputed to have been planted by him.

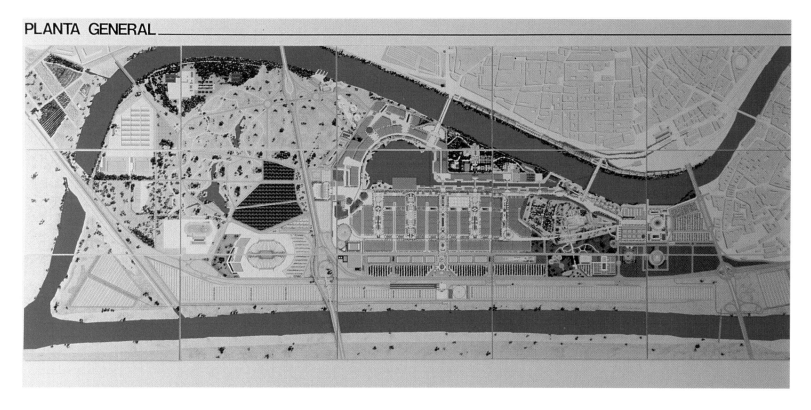

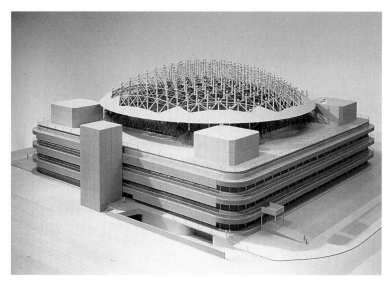

Top *Overall plan for the World Expo site, showing the normal course of the Guadalquivir River at the bottom. The huge wooded area to the left will become a recreational park; car parking is along the straight stretch of the river.*

Above *Model for the sports hall of the Barcelona Olympics, designed by Japanese designer Arata Isozaki. The extraordinary domed roof was lowered into place by cranes when the building was completed.*

Over the course of the years the river, which once flowed on both sides of the island, began to slow down and falter on the northern stretch, finally leaving a series of ox-bows. The southern stretch was still navigable, a busy waterway from the Port of Seville down to the sea, as it is to this day. In the 1850s, an Englishman called Charles Pickman bought the now disused island site and built a factory to make ceramics, using local skills. This small industry was carried on by his family until the 1970s, when it moved to Jerez, and in 1987 the island was bought by the state from the Pickman family specifically to be used for the Expo.

An international competition was set up for the design of the site. Part of the plans laid down will involve reopening the northern stretch for at least the six-month period of the Expo, to make it a useful additional method of transport to and from the site. The competition was won by the US-based Italian architect, Emilio Ambasz, whose design featured a series of lakes off the main river, with many of the pavilions projecting into the water. However, it was felt that this concept, although imaginative, did not make sufficient allowance for the scorching Andalucian summer sun, so the organizers employed a team of architects who finally came up with a design using some elements of the prize-winning design and some from other entries. This includes shady walks and ingenious water systems for cooling and circulation of air.

The Expo will open on Easter Monday and close on 12 October, the 500th anniversary of the discovery of the New World. Discoveries (Los Descubrimientos) is the theme of the Expo, and La Avenida de los

PLANNING THE FUTURE

Descubrimientos, which runs from one side of the site to the other, will be devoted to history. The easternmost point of the site, housing administrative buildings and a large open amphitheatre, is to be the venue for the main ceremonies and sports arenas. The conference centre and hub of the Expo will be in the ancient walled area of the monastery itself, whose former orchards are being transformed into gardens. Both the monastery buildings and the interesting pointed chimneys of the old ceramics factory are to be restored, as is the paved courtyard which holds Columbus' baobab tree.

There are to be almost 100 pavilions, over 80 of which will be dedicated to participating countries, with others covering individual themes, such as conservation, energy and the arts. They are to be positioned along wide avenues, where hundreds of mature trees have been transplanted, growing at three heights to give maximum protection from the sun. There are covered walkways and complex arrangements of fountains, pools and cascades. Water, the Moors' favourite air-cooling system, has been used in various clever and inventive ways. In some places its flow is directed underneath porous blocks, chilling the pavements and hence the air above, while in others air flow is fanned through series of fountains to cool, circulate and revitalize it.

A huge semi-circular lake has been created from an existing smaller one, with a long canal leading to it, where boating will take place, and earth from the excavation has been used to build a large open-air auditorium. The main Spanish pavilion and separate buildings for each autonomous region of Spain are on the shores of the lake, with a promenade running in front. There are also a Park of the Future, an amusement park, and large formal gardens. Entertainments, firework displays and cultural events put on by participating countries will be held into the night.

Transport around the site will be by foot, small buses or boat, with a cable-car and monorail to provide panoramic views. Transport to the site has been planned with meticulous care, and a new railway line direct from Madrid is being built which can carry high-speed trains. This will cross the river over a new bridge and stop right next to the site. At the busiest times there will be ten trains an hour arriving there, six of them through from Madrid. The airport capacities of Seville, Jerez and Málaga are all being doubled, with Jerez achieving international status for the first time. Motorways, providing better links between Seville and the north as well as providing faster travel east and west across Andalucía, are also being built.

Perhaps the most exciting and ambitious aspect of the new transport facilities is the building of seven new bridges across the Guadalquivir. The largest, the Puente del Batán, costing some ten billion pesetas, and with two traffic lanes in each direction, has been designed by José Antonio Fernández Ordóñez. Another, by Fernández Casado, has two levels, one for trains and the other a six-lane road for motor vehicles. This will be built in local shipyards and floated down to its position. The Puente de Chapina will form the new access from Huelva and

A centuries-old olive tree stands guard in front of the group of buildings known as El Recinto de la Cartuja. Where possible, the trees from an ancient olive grove are being preserved; many thousands of mature trees are also being transplanted there. The ancient convent buildings are being restored, and used both as a tourist attraction and for administrative offices.

PLANNING THE FUTURE

Extremadura in the west. Designed by José Luís Manzanares, it is inspired by the Pont d'Alexandre III in Paris, built for the Universal Exposition of 1900. The Pasarela de la Cartuja, by a German engineering company, sets a new world record for its lightness in relation to its span. The Puente de la Barqueta, built on floating pontoons in the shape of aeroplane wings, is both aesthetically pleasing and practical in economic terms, as it does not have to be permanent. Finally, there is the Autovía San Lázaro-Camas, a massive viaduct crossing the island from east to west. This has two symmetrical bridges on either side, each with one pylon on the island whose supports project right across the river. Designed by the architect Santiago Calatrava, who produced for Barcelona a bridge that verges on sculpture, this promises to be the most spectacular of all.

The complex satellite and communications network being set up for 1992 will be of tremendous benefit after the Expo, when the final firework has fizzled out. The whole project has been planned so that, when the last of the expected 18 million visitors have finally packed their bags, the ancient site of La Cartuja will be ready for 1993 and beyond. The Discoveries Pavilion (Pabellon de los Descubrimientos) will become a permanent centre of science and technology, while others have already been earmarked to house technological faculties of Seville university, ministries, research institutes and high-tech factories. IBM, one of the exhibitors, has pledged to maintain a permanent exhibition centre, and other major participants are expected to follow suit. The conference centre will also be a permanent feature.

MADRID

Madrid has been running various rehabilitation projects since the late '70s, with improvements to road transport, updating of housing and cultural facilities made more accessible to a wider public by enlarging premises or taking over new ones, often in historic buildings. For 1992, when the city will be the European Cultural Capital of the Year, more ambitious schemes have been put into effect. Land formerly in public ownership is being sold to provide space for urban development, one of the aims of this being to hold land prices steady in the years preceding 1992. There will be a huge international fair and conference centre, with hotels and other services, between Madrid and Barajas airport, and a Port of Madrid for road transporters is being built on the new fourth ring road. This will also have hotels and services as well as a transport centre which is intended to decrease the number of lorries coming into the city, thus relieving serious traffic problems. With the third and fourth ring roads complete, the fifth and sixth ring roads are also under construction.

The most imaginative plan is the creation of a 'green corridor' (El Pasillo Verde). A railway line which crosses Madrid from the Principe Pío to Atocha stations is to be sunk below ground. The strip previously occupied by the railway lines will become a new main road, while the land surrounding it will be used for parks, sports arenas, housing, offices and water-treatment works. The creation of these and the various arts and cultural centres mentioned elsewhere in this book will guarantee a lively year for Madrid, as well as better-organized traffic and transport systems for the future.

BARCELONA

Cities which host the Olympic Games always take the opportunity to give themselves a face lift, but the scale of the projects being undertaken in Barcelona is staggering, as are the high standards the organizers have set themselves under the leadership of the mayor and Olympic chairman, Pasqual Maragall. There are major urban schemes to improve the environment, ease traffic problems, and clean up and revitalize the working-class suburbs. Public housing is being refurbished, and quantities of new squares and parks provided. The city has been given a public identity, with consciousness-raising campaigns employing eye-catching graphics and slogans on posters and banners. The build-up to 1992 began in earnest in 1987.

There are four main Olympic areas, deliberately sited in different quarters of Barcelona so that no one part of the city will benefit more than another. Ring roads and new public transport systems will connect all the four sites, the aim being that none should be more than 20 minutes from another by public transport. The four areas are Montjuïc Park, Diagonal, Hebron Valley and the Parc de Mar ('Seaside Park'). Montjuïc is the main one, a vast wooded park on a steep hill overlooking the city, whose existing gardens – both formal and informal – were becoming a little run down. This was the site of the many pavilions of the 1929 International Exhibition, most of which were dismantled the following year. It contains many varied attractions, such as the impressive Miró Foundation, various museums, a Greek amphitheatre and an amusement park, while the famous Hollywood Deco-style cascades still dance to the sound of concerts put on at weekends. Terrifying funiculars reach the peaks, one from the docks passing perilously high over the sea.

A stadium built in 1929 on Montjuïc's summit is now being completely transformed by architect Federico Correa, but its original façade will be retained. Its depth doubled, it will be the main Olympic stadium for several of the major activities and for the opening and closing events. Facilities for the athletes are housed beneath the stands. Next to this is the Sant Jordi Palace gymnasium, holding 17,000 people, which has been designed by Japanese architect Arata Isozaki. The massive canopy-like roof is to be assembled on the ground and hoisted into position by cranes. Nearby is the INEF Pavilion, designed by Ricardo Bofill in Neoclassical style; this will later become the home of the permanent Sports University. Bofill has also designed a hotel in a similar style. Some of the swimming pools and sports palaces are also to be sited near the Montjuïc summit. One of the most technically sophisticated designs is that for the Press Centre, where every journalist will have access to videotext information and direct links to their home bases by means of fibre-optics. High-definition television and interactive video

PLANNING THE FUTURE

will also be offered. The design of the communications tower, to be built on Tibidabo Mountain, went out to international competition, and was eventually won by the British architect Norman Foster. Most of these architectural gems are within a discus throw of the reconstruction of Mies van der Rohe's famous German pavilion for the 1929 Expo. All the projects should be completed well before 1992, so that they are thoroughly tested and any problems ironed out before the events.

The Diagonal site, which includes Barcelona's beloved Football Club stadium, holding 120,000 people, is to be improved and enlarged, with additional provisions for visitors, and will host Olympic football, judo and, at the neighbouring Polo Club, tennis and horse trials. The Hebron Valley area already has a velodrome which hosts world-class cycling competitions. Handball and field sports events, as well as the Youth Camp for young visitors and volunteers, will all be there. This is all part of a larger scheme for updating this part of the city.

The Parc de Mar must be the most ambitious project of all. This was the birthplace of Barcelona's industry, and hence Spain's industrial revolution, in the nineteenth century. Much of the privately owned site had become either run down or derelict; it is all now publicly owned, and an ambitious scheme by Barcelona's favourite architect Oriol Bohigas and his team has been put into effect. Existing factories have been resited

ABOVE *The sports hall by Arata Isozaki, for the Barcelona Olympics, almost complete. This is situated on top of the hills of Montjuïc park, across a wide paved piazza from the main stadium.*

LEFT *The main Olympic stadium, built in 1929, restored and altered drastically by Federico Correa. The Olympic ring is on newly excavated ground, making the stadium twice as deep as previously.*

elsewhere, and the main sewage works is to be moved in its entirety. In 1990 the long-standing problem of lack of sea access will be solved by partially submerging the main railway line, which runs the length of the site. All this will completely clear the site in readiness for the building of the Olympic village. The emphasis of the plan has been placed on its later use as public and private housing, which the architects see as a revival of the spirit of nineteenth-century Socialism. There are to be 6000 apartments and two skyscrapers, while a continuation of the ring road will run between the village and the sea, most of it underground. The needs of the Olympics participants will be well catered for in 1992, but the planners' sights are set on 1993 and the twenty-first century.

The street layout of other parts of Barcelona, which was laid down in the last century, is being continued here, with the provision of many large squares and gardens. This is the particular responsibility of architect Beth Galí, who is also in charge of all the architectural elements of the Olympics. One of her principles is to allow as much diversity as possible while retaining common elements throughout Barcelona, so the street furniture and fittings designed for the Parc de Mar will be repeated or echoed on other Olympic sites as well as areas of the city currently being refurbished. Alongside the Parc de Mar will be a new port and marina, where the sailing competitions will be held, with a newly created island

site for conferences. A broad esplanade will run virtually the whole length of the shore; major traffic routes have been moved out of sight, and car parks are being built below ground. The Paseo Maritimo at Moll de la Fusta ('Wood Dock'), where there was until recently a timber-shipping business, is already a new focal point for the city, with its imaginative restaurants designed by star architects. Covered walkways to protect visitors from the hot summer sun, with fountains, pools and drinking fountains are already completed or in the pipeline. Everything from rubbish bins to decorative paving stones has been taken into account.

The telecommunications side has been planned by BIT '92 (Barcelona Informática y Telecomunicaciones). Part of their brief is to produce a system able to accommodate any new technology that may be developed up to a few months before the opening of the Olympics, which has involved close collaboration with various telecommunications companies. This is vital to the project, and ideas have been presented during conferences with Siemens, Xerox, IBM, Philips, Olivetti and Apple, among others. International companies were invited to tender for different areas, but only if they already had a headquarters in Spain. The Olympic Committee foresees a tremendous potential boost Barcelona's future as an international technological centre.

An award-winning poster in the graphics competition, by Salvador Saura and Ramón Torrente, an evocative illustration using trainer footprints.

201

PLANNING THE FUTURE

CHRONOLOGY

100 YEARS OF SPANISH DESIGN AND ARCHITECTURE

1884 Crypt and apse completed of the church of La Sagrada Familia, Antoni Gaudí's best known and wildly ambitious project, still under construction.

1888 Universal Exhibition of Barcelona takes place at a period of great economic growth, but continuous political upheavals.

1896 Completion of Els Quatre Gats, the famous restaurant frequented by Barcelona's artistic community: architect Josep Puig í Cadalfalch.

1900 Construction of Casa Amatller, private residence (now a museum) and complete interior scheme by architect Josep Puig í Cadalfalch.

1903 Fomento de las Artes Decorativas (FAD), an association to encourage the decorative arts, founded in Barcelona.

1905/8 Palau de la Música Catalana concert hall completed in the highly decorated style of the period, architect Lluís Doménech í Montaner.

1906 Casa Battló completed, for which architect Antoni Gaudí also designed interiors and furniture, now a museum.

1908 Completion of Fabbrica Aymerich, with its extraordinary roof of pointed eaves, architect Lluís Moncunill í Parellada.

1910 La Pedrera (The Stone Quarry) apartment block, Barcelona, completed; architect Antoni Gaudí.

1914 First phase of the Parque Güell completed, with its chapel, walls, seating and landscaping plan, architect Antoni Gaudí. A second phase, including craftsman's cottages and studios, to Gaudí's eternal disappointment, was never begun.

1929 International Exhibition of Barcelona; Mies van der Rohe Pavilion completed. While this was the emblem of Modernism, the FAD in Barcelona was totally opposed to its austerity and what they saw as stylistic poverty. The Barcelona chair designed for it is perhaps one of the best known chairs ever.

1929 'Generation of '29' group of artists formed, often meeting at Els Quatre Gats. Includes Salvador Dali, Federico García Lorca, Luís Buñuel.

1930 Creation of modernist architect groups GATPAC in Barcelona and GATEPAC in Zaragoza.

1936/39 Spanish Civil War, half a million die, many more leave the country.

1937 Cristóbal Balenciaga leaves Spain to set up in Paris; joins Pablo Picasso and other Spanish exiles.

1956 André Ricard contacts ASID (American Society of Industrial Designers) in the US. The first Spanish industrial designer to form links with the USA, he strikes up a friendship with Raymond Loewy, one of the founding fathers of US industrial design.

1957 IDIB (Instituto de Diseño Industrial de Barcelona) set up to coordinate industrial design.

1959 Massana School in Barcelona begins teaching graphic design, first such course in Spain.

1960s Industrial and building boom, tourism boom follows abolition of visa requirements for foreigners.

1960 ADIFAD (Agrupación de Diseño Industrial del Fomento de las Artes Decorativas) founded in Barcelona.

1961 ADIFAD accepted as member of ICSID (International Congress of Societies of Industrial Design).
Delta Prizes created by ADIFAD.
ADGFAD (Agrupación de Diseño Gráfico del Fomento de las Artes Decorativas) founded. Elisava Design School founded in Barcelona.

1963 André Ricard elected vice-president of ICSID, first Spanish designer to take an active role in international design affairs.

1964 Eina Design School founded in Barcelona. LAUS prizes created for graphic design by ADGFAD.

1965 Industrial design department founded at Massana.

1970s Energy crisis begins to bite, recession starts.

1971 As a measure of a budding respect for Spanish designers, the ICSID congress is held in Ibiza.

1972 Cristóbal Balenciaga dies.

1973 BCD (Barcelona Centro de Diseño) founded.

1974/80 Marne-La-Vallée, a huge post-modern public housing complex, constructed in Paris, architect Ricardo Bofill.

1975 Another early post-modern project, La Casa en la Isla de Pantellería completed, architects Oscar Tusquets and Lluís Clotet.

1976 Bankinter building completed, one of the first 'high tech' office buildings, but with distinctively Spanish forms; architects Ramón Bescos and Rafael Moneo.

1976/81 Colegio de Arquitectos, Seville, completed architects Enrique Perea and Gabriel Ruíz Cabrera.

1977 BCD mark of quality for Spanish products created, on the same lines as the British Design Council kite mark.

1978 Parc de la Marca Hispánica, huge monumental park close to the French border, architect Ricardo Bofill.

ADP (Asociación de Diseñadores Profesionales) founded in Barcelona.

1980 Centro de Arte Reina Sofía, work begins under architect Antonio Fernández Alba.

1982 'Diseño Diseño' exhibition organised by BCD, funded by Ministry of Industry and Energy, shown to the people of Barcelona.

1983 Roberto Verinno opens fashion shop in Paris, first designer to do so.

Sybilla presents first fashion collection in Madrid.

1984 La Movida, the Madrid arts movement covering music, fine art, fashion and film-making, in full swing.

Escuela Gravina, Valencia, completed in a monumental style similar to that of Le Corbusier, architect Portaceli.

1985 Museo Nacional de Arte Romano, Mérida, completed, architect Rafael Moneo.

Pedro Almodóvar's film *Matador* receives international acclaim, Almodóvar uses stars of La Movida and avant-garde Spanish designers for sets and costumes.

San Fermín School completed, Madrid, architect Alberto Campo Baeza.

ADIFAD given Gold medal of Bellas Artes by HM King Juan Carlos.
CAD/CAM centre opens at BCD.
'Diseño España – Europalia' exhibition held in Brussels, organised by ADIFAD, ADGFAD, ADP and BCD, funded by Ministry of Industry and Energy.

1986 Spanish fashion jewellery exports up by 73 per cent.

'Diseño en España' exhibition held in Madrid at Centro de Arte Reina Sofía, funded by Ministry of Industry and Energy.

1987 El Palau de la Musicá, Valencia, completed, architect José María García de Paredes. Now regarded as one of the world's best concert halls.

Casa G Hidalgo, Allela, completed, architects Jordi Garcés and Enric Sória.

Cristóbal Balenciaga National Fashion Prizes instituted by Ministry of Industry and Energy.

1988 Casa Gay, Barcelona, completed, architects Antoní de Moragas and Irene Sánchez-Hernando.

Casa Turegano completed in Madrid, architect Alberto Campo Baeza.

Adolfo Dominguez has 300 fashion shops in Spain, 100 more worldwide.

Complete reorganization of the barely finished Centro de Arte Reina Sofía in Madrid, to much public criticism and press controversy.

1989 Pedro Almodóvar's film, *Women on the Verge of a Nervous Breakdown*, has several Oscar nominations.

BIBLIOGRAPHY

Architettura Modernista: Gaudí e il movimiento catalano, Oriol Bohigas (Einaudi Editore, Italy, 1968)

Arquitectura Española, años 50 – años 80, Antón Capitel (Mopu Arquitectura, Spain, 1986)

Arquitectura Española Contemporanea, Eduard Bru and José-Luís Mateo (Gustavo Gili, Spain, 1984)

Arquitectura Española Contemporanea, Luís Domènech Girban (Editorial Blume, Spain, 1986)

ARDI magazine, publishers Grupo Zeta, Barcelona

Arena magazine, publishers Producciones del Desierto, Madrid

Art Book I and *II,* ed. Agustín Norberto Calabró (Editorial Pigmalión, Spain, 1985)

Bach/Mora, Vittorio Savi (Gustavo Gili, Spain, 1987)

Ricardo Bofill: L'Architecture d'un Homme, François Hébert-Stevens (Librairie Arthaud, France, 1978)

Comedores, Luís de Candamo (Editorial Cigueña, 1950)

Contemporary Spanish Architecture: an Eclectic Panorama, ed. Ignacio Solá-Morales (Rizzoli, USA, 1986)

Diseño de Arquitectos en los 80, Juli Capella and Quim Larrea (Gustavo Gili, Spain, 1987)

El Diseño en España (Ministry of Industry and Energy exhibition catalogue, 1985)

Design In Catalonia (Barcelona Centro de Diseño, Ministry of Industry and Energy, Spain, 1988)

La Destrucción de Obras de Arte en España (San Sebastián: Instituto de España, Spain, 1938)

The Dominance of Spain 1550–1660, Brian Reade (Harrap, UK, 1951)

Dormitorios, Juan Lafora (Editorial Cigueña, Spain, 1950)

DTI: Spain Country Profile (Department of Trade and Industry, UK, 1988)

La Estetica del Vestir Clasico, ed. Pedro Roca Piñol (Colección Literaria Dedicada al Traje, Terrasa, Spain, 1942)

Franco y La Cultura (Madrid: Oficina de Información Española, Spain, 1947)

Garcés/Soría, Oriol Bohigas (Gustavo Gili, Spain, 1987)

Homage to Barcelona, the City and its Art (Arts Council of Great Britain, UK, 1986)

El Mueble Español en los Siglos XV, XVI and XVII; El Mueble Romantico; Antología de la Silla Española, all by Afridisio Aguado

Muebles de Estilo Español, Marqués de Lozoya and José Claret Rubira (Gustavo Gili, Spain, 1962)

Modern Architecture in Colour, Werner Hoffman and Udo Kultermann (Thames and Hudson, UK, 1970)

Pintura Española, Siglos XVI–XVII (Museo del Prado, Spain)

Alla ricerca di un'architettura nazionale, Lluís Domènech í Montaner (Las Renaixenca, Italy, 1878)

La Seda en La Indumentaria, Siglos XVI–XIX (Palacio de Comillas, Barcelona, 1957)

Spain 1808–1975, Raymond Carr (Oxford University Press, 1982)

Spain: El Fascismo intenta destruir el Museo del Prado (Army, 5th Regiment, Spain, 1947)

The Spaniards, John Hooper (Viking Penguin Books, UK, 1986)

Sur Exprés magazine, publishers Producciones del Desierto, Madrid

Young Spanish Architecture, Alberto Campo Baeza and Charles Poisay (Ark Monograph, Spain, 1985)

INDEX

Page numbers in *italics* indicate the sites of relevant captions.

207

Photographic Acknowledgements

Architectural Association 27, 39, 46; Bridgeman Art Library titlepage 8, 12, 13 left, 13 right, 14, 21, 106; Juli Capella and Quim Larrea 32, 33, 47, 58, 59, 60 left, 62, 63, 64, 65 top, 65 bottom, 66, 67 left, 67 right; Lluis Casals 6, 26, 28, 29, 30, 31 top, 31 bottom; COOB '92, SA 192, 202 top, 202 bottom; Emma Dent Coad 16 centre, 16 right, 17 left, 17 right, 18 left, 18 right, 19, 22, 23 left, 23 right, 34, 35, 37, 42, 45, 48, 49, 50 top, 50 bottom, 53, 54, 55, 56, 57, 60 top right, 60 bottom left, 61, 68, 78, 79, 80, 81 left, 81 right, 82, 83, 84, 85 left, 85 right, 86, 87, 89 left, 89 right, 90, 91, 92, 93 top left, 93 bottom left, 93 right, 94, 95 left, 95 right, 96, 97 left, 97 right, 98, 99, 100 left, 100 right, 101, 102, 103, 105 left, 105 right, 109, 110, 111, 112 top, 112 bottom, 113 top, 113 bottom, 114 top, 114 bottom, 115, 116, 117, 118, 119, 120, 121, 122, 123 top, 123 centre, 123 bottom, 124 top, 124 bottom, 125 top, 125 bottom, 126 left, 126 right, 127, 128, 129, 130 left, 130 right, 131, 134, 135, 140, 141, 142, 143 left, 143 right, 144, 145 left, 145 right, 146, 147 left, 147 right, 148, 149, 150, 151, 152, 153 left, 153 right, 155 left, 155 right, 156, 157 left, 157 right, 159, 160, 161, 163 left, 163 right, 164, 165, 166, 167, 168, 169 top, 169 bottom, 170, 173, 175, 176, 177 top, 177 bottom, 178, 179 left, 179 right, 180, 181, 182, 183, 184, 185 left, 185 right, 186, 187, 188, 189 left, 189 right, 190, 191 top, 191 bottom, 194 right, 201; Nieves Fernandez 132; Galeria Mar Estrada 70; Kobal Collection 15; Mas 136, 139 left, 139 right; Mas/Ricardo Bofill half-title page, 40, 41 top, 41 bottom; Spectrum Colour Library 73, 74, 75; Frank Spooner 77; Oscar Tusquets Blanca and Lluis Clotet 44; World Exp '92 194 left, 195 top, 195 bottom, 197, 198; ZEFA Picture Library (UK) 10, 24 top, 24 bottom.

© ADAGP, Paris and DACS London 1990 4, 14; © DACS 1990 13 left, 13 right, 106; © DEMART PRO ARTE BV 8.